Unwavering

Learning to Do the Next Right Thing in Your Walk with God

Margo Fieseler

WESTBOW PRESS
A DIVISION OF THOMAS NELSON
& ZONDERVAN

Copyright © 2018 Margo Fieseler.

All rights reserved. No part of this book may be used or reproduced by any means, graphic, electronic, or mechanical, including photocopying, recording, taping or by any information storage retrieval system without the written permission of the author except in the case of brief quotations embodied in critical articles and reviews.

This book is a work of non-fiction. Unless otherwise noted, the author and the publisher make no explicit guarantees as to the accuracy of the information contained in this book and in some cases, names of people and places have been altered to protect their privacy. This work is based on the experiences of an individual. Every effort has been made to ensure the accuracy of the content.

Contributing Editor: Reji Laberje
Interior Design Elements: Sarah Rickaby
Cover Design: Sarah Rickaby
Author Photo: Paul Moroder of Moroder Photography

WestBow Press books may be ordered through booksellers or by contacting:

WestBow Press
A Division of Thomas Nelson & Zondervan
1663 Liberty Drive
Bloomington, IN 47403
www.westbowpress.com
1 (866) 928-1240

Because of the dynamic nature of the Internet, any web addresses or links contained in this book may have changed since publication and may no longer be valid. The views expressed in this work are solely those of the author and do not necessarily reflect the views of the publisher, and the publisher hereby disclaims any responsibility for them.

Any people depicted in stock imagery provided by Getty Images are models, and such images are being used for illustrative purposes only. Certain stock imagery © Getty Images.

ISBN: 978-1-9736-3579-6 (sc)
ISBN: 978-1-9736-3578-9 (hc)
ISBN: 978-1-9736-3580-2 (e)

Library of Congress Control Number: 2018909145

Print information available on the last page.

WestBow Press rev. date: 08/27/2018

Quantity order requests can be emailed to Unwavering@margofieseler.com

Scripture quotations marked "AMP" are taken from *The Amplified Bible* of 2015 (AMP) Copyright © 2015 by The Lockman Foundation, La Habra, CA 90631. Used with permission. All rights reserved.

Scripture quotations marked "ESV" are taken from The Holy Bible, English Standard Version). Copyright © 2001 by Crossway Bibles, a division of Good News Publishers. Used with permission. All rights reserved.

Scripture quotations marked "KJV" are taken from the King James Version of the Bible, which is in the public domain.

Scripture quotations marked "MSG" are taken from THE MESSAGE. Copyright © by Eugene H. Peterson 1993, 1994, 1995, 1996, 2000, 2001, 2002. Used by permission of NavPress Publishing Group.

Scripture quotations marked "NIV" are taken from the *Holy Bible, New International Version®. NIV®.* Copyright © 1973, 1978, 1984, and 2011 by Biblica, Inc. Used by permission. All rights reserved worldwide.

Scripture quotations marked "NLT" are taken from the *Holy Bible, New Living Translation,* copyright © 1996, 2004, 2015. Used by permission of Tyndale House Publishers, Inc., Carol Stream, IL 60188 USA. All rights reserved.

Scripture quotations marked "NKJV" are taken from the New King James Version. Copyright © 1982 by Thomas Nelson, Inc. Used with permission. All rights reserved.

Contents

Prologue: Someday xi

Chapter 1 I Got This 1
  Devotions: God's Pursuit of Me 7

Chapter 2 Um ... Not So Much 20
  Devotions: Conviction 30

Chapter 3 What Took You So Long? 44
  Devotions: No More Detours Away from the Heart of God 50

Chapter 4 Squeegee the Shower 62
  Devotions: Learning to Obey 70

Chapter 5 God Always Has "Plan A" 82
  Devotions: God is Good...All the Time 93

Chapter 6 Trusting the Unseen 104
  Devotions: Always for My Good and His Glory ... 115

Chapter 7 Less like My Putrid Self 126
  Devotions: God's Purifying Process 134

Chapter 8 I *Am* Fit 146
  Devotions: I'm an Overcomer 158

Chapter 9 Highly Favored, Richly Blessed 170
  Devotions: My Identity in Christ 178

Chapter 10 Knowing Jesus 191
  Devotions: Standing on His Promises 197

Addendum 213
About Margo Fieseler 217

This book is dedicated to my mom, who gave away her life so I could find mine.

Prologue

Someday

Today is my someday.

For years, I've been asked, "When are you writing your book?"

My tummy would roll around, my mind would fuzz, and I'd stare blankly, answering, "Someday."

Today is my someday.

I used to imagine myself seated in an overstuffed chair, curled up in a blanket, my collie at my feet, and sipping a cup of English breakfast tea. Meanwhile inspirational verbiage flowed through my fingertips as I clicked away on my laptop. Of course, my location would be idyllic, like a well-appointed she shed, a lakefront cabin, or a twentieth-floor balcony overlooking the Mediterranean.

Only when I finally took my focus off all the externals so I could write the perfect book and started asking God to reveal His plan, way, and timing did my someday come.

This book isn't intended to highlight my adventures. Rather, my impassioned prayer is that somehow, someway, God is using a broken vessel like me to share His life-changing love, grace, mercy, and power.

If He can radically rescue, restore, and release me to be about His kingdom work, then He can do the same for you.

When your steps with God become unwavering, doing the next right thing with Him is as natural as walking. Oh, you might trudge through mud at times or hike up some slippery slopes, *but God* (my two favorite words) will always hold your hand.

Don't let go of His grip.

Join me on the best adventure ever as I learned to "do the next right thing" in my daily walk with God. He promises it will be worth it.

You'll find, woven into a true narrative, a total of fifty-two devotionals to gently guide you along a path of doing the next right thing with God.

Read them again and again. Do a few at a time, pick the ones that most call to you, or absorb them as you follow the story. Journal your unwavering thoughts. They are God's Word that spoke aloud as I learned to do my next right thing in my walk with Him. I pray that you, too, will hear Him as your steps become unwavering.

By the way, two externals were constant while I was birthing this book.
1. Sipping English breakfast tea
2. Petting my faithful collie at my side

Chapter 1

I Got This

Mom. It all started with my mom.

I know what you're thinking: *Well, of course it did, Margo; after all, she carried and birthed you.*

They're not just the physical beginnings I mean, though. They are more than that. They are the emotional, mental, and spiritual beginnings that came from my mom. My mom affected every portion of my heart, soul, mind, and strength—for good. At the time, I didn't always think her influence was for my good, but through the years that truth has become very evident.

During my birth, I was already in trouble. My umbilical cord was tightly wound around my neck. As the obstetrician went into rescue mode, my mom trusted God for the outcome. She proclaimed a verse she had committed to memory from her King James Bible. "A merry heart doeth good like a medicine, but a broken spirit drieth the bones" (Proverbs 17:22 KJV).

That's who my mom turned to first—God and His Word, the Bible—no matter what life circumstance bumped into her. Instead of the normal crying out in physical pain during labor and delivery, she cried out to her personal God. Later in life, I thought, *How odd that that was the verse spoken over me.* I would have rushed to a portion of scripture to help or comfort me, such as "Do not fear, for I am with you; do not be dismayed, for I am your God. I will strengthen you and help you; I will uphold you with my righteous right hand" (Isaiah 41:10 NIV).

But no! Mom's focus was on me—this little baby she hadn't met yet but whom she loved with all her momma's heart.

She prayed for me.

She didn't pray for her welfare or for the easing of her pain but for her child's heart. She prayed that, through all the turbulence of breaking into this world, my heart (mind, will, and emotions) would be blessed by the one who'd created me—the one who had already ordained every day before even one of them had come to be. "My frame was not hidden from you when I was made in the secret place, when I was woven together in the depths of the earth. Your eyes saw my unformed body; all the days ordained for me were written in your book before one of them came to be" (Psalm 139:15–16 NIV).

> When life bumps into you, it's what's already inside that spills out.

Mom taught me that when life bumps into you, it's what's already inside that spills out. Mom would hold a glass of water and ask, "Margo, what's gonna spill out of this glass if I bump into it?"

I answered, "Water."

"That's right, honey, because water is already inside that glass." Her eyes twinkled, and her mouth curved upward as she placed her hand on mine as if to say, *Be careful what you fill yourself with.*

And when life bumped, jarred, or blasted into her, it was evident to all that she would overflow with Jesus.

His power.
His wisdom.
His strength.
His authority.
His love.
His mercy.
His grace.
His peace.

Through it all, mom would walk in JOY. How? She chose to put

Jesus first,
Others second, and
Yourself (herself) dead last.

If only I would have listened. I was being given wisdom that was pure and peace loving right from above through my precious, God-given mom. Mom was not only beautiful on the inside but also drop-dead gorgeous on the outside. She had huge brown eyes you could sink right into. People automatically were drawn to her. I loved being around her.

We had so much together time since my two sisters, Marcia and Marilyn (my dad called us the "3M Sisters"), were ten and eleven years older than I. While my siblings were already attending college and making wedding plans, Mom was teaching a Good

News Club in our home and sharing the gospel with other kids in the neighborhood.

My friends hung on her every word as though she were the pied piper. "Mrs. Lance, Mrs. Lance!" they'd call out.

Mom lightened up the room and served her famous stove-top popcorn to grubby, little outstretched hands. Sometimes my friends chatted more with her than with me because she continually poured herself into them.

I wanted to be like my mom.

No matter who came over, they loved her. I was so proud, but I never wanted to accept the fact that it was Jesus who had made her like that.

That's when she'd tenderly turn to me and whisper, "You're missing out on God's best for you right now, honey."

Then she'd wander off, singing. Yes, singing in her glorious soprano voice. She and her twin, Margaret, had been a harmonizing duo throughout their younger years, so all her favorite old hymns—"His Eye Is on the Sparrow," "Great Is Thy Faithfulness," "How Great Thou Art," and "Turn Your Eyes upon Jesus"—would burst forth from her lips. Even when she upset me with a firm voice (a rare thing that came only when I deserved it), she came back later and apologized. Seriously? Even now?

I used to think (even though I knew it was impossible) that if God could have picked a wife, it would have been my mom.

As I approached my college years, my own wisdom seemed so much better than Mom's (or God's). It was so much more fun.

I had always heard my pastor, Sunday school teacher, vacation Bible school helper, and Youth for Christ (today called CRU) leader share the same godly wisdom, but my way seemed better. That was the problem. It only *seemed* better. I should have heeded God's wisdom, but instead I declared to all those around me, "I got this."

"The way of fools seem right to them, but the wise listen to advice" (Proverbs 12:15 NIV). I definitely played the fool. So onward I coursed my way, proclaiming, "I got this." Even if I was sinking or stinking it up, I'd push ahead full speed.

All the while, my precious mom prayed.

"Lord, don't give Margo any peace until the peace of Jesus rests in her." So God was on the hunt to capture my heart, as she had prayed even before I was born.

The Hound of Heaven: Jesus. Always pursuing me. Always coming after me. Always wanting me. It was I who continued to avoid, evade, and keep on the wrong road for years. Thankfully, He never gave up on me. (Actually, He can't. He's God. It's not His nature to give up on us.)

> God was on the hunt to capture my heart even before I was born.

And Mom prayed on.

Throughout my college and young adult years, I was full of defiance, disrespect, and disobedience. Her faithfulness to God's promises never wavered. And God heard her cry—not in her timing or in her way, but nevertheless she clung to His promises. Mom stood on them.

I can hear Mom's lilting soprano voice even now, singing,

> Standing on the promises of Christ my King,
> Through eternal ages let His praises ring.
> Glory in the highest, I will shout and sing.
> Standing on the promises of God.

The song went on.
The song of God.
The song of Mom.
My mom.

Father God, thank You for choosing my mom just for me, a mom who would give her life away so I could find mine. Year after year after year, she never stopped trusting Your best plan for me. I am forever grateful.

And thank You, Jesus, that there is always someone standing in the gap, even when we stubbornly go our own putrid way, proclaiming, "I got this."

You pursue us, even when we try to ignore Your outpouring, sacrificial love. I'm so grateful You're the Hound of Heaven, who is always coming after us in Your loving-kindness.

Devotions
for Your Next Right Steps

God's Pursuit of Me

Breathtaking Life
Don't Miss Out!
Simple. Profound. Life Changing.
Just Answer the Door
Right Thinking

Breathtaking Life

Oh yes, you shaped me first inside, then out; you formed me in my mother's womb. I thank you, High God—you're breathtaking! Body and soul, I am marvelously made! I worship in adoration—what a creation! You know me inside and out, know every bone in my body; You know exactly how I was made, bit by bit, how I was sculpted from nothing into something. Like an open book, you watched me grow from conception to birth; all the stages of my life were spread out before you. The days of my life all prepared before I'd even lived one day.

—Psalm 139:13–16 (MSG)

The maker of heaven and earth made you.
Made me.
Made every detail.
The one who flung the stars in place. The one who orders the heavens—shaped me. Seriously? (Steep in that reality for a moment.)

> Someone knows you more intimately than you know yourself.

"He speaks to the sun and it does not shine; he seals off the light of the stars He alone stretches out the heavens and treads on the waves of the sea. He is the Maker of the Bear and Orion, the Pleiades and the constellations of the south. He performs wonders that cannot be fathomed, miracles that cannot be counted" (Job 9:7–10 NIV). That same almighty God reached down and intricately formed me in my mother's womb. Bit by bit, He sculpted me from nothing into something. He knows every bone in my body. He knows me inside and out. More than I know myself, He knows me.

Doesn't that truth stop you in your tracks?

Someone knows you more intimately than you know yourself. Even from conception to birth, He watched you grow.

Your entire span of life is spread before Him like an open book. Every day of your life has been ordained before one of them has come to be.

As the all-knowing (omniscient) God, seeing your days is a piece of cake for Him. He knows the end from the beginning. He wrote the final chapter of your "book of life" before you even began it.

So if this all-knowing, Creator God made you—and He did—and if this omniscient God knows you inside and out—and He does—should truth compel you to know Him more than you know yourself? He's got the inside scoop on your whole life.

**We should exclaim as the psalmist,
"I thank you, High God.
You're breathtaking!"**

Don't Miss Out!

God doesn't treat us as our sins deserve, nor pay us back in-full for our wrongs. As high as heaven is over the earth, so strong is his love to those who fear him. And as far as sunrise is from sunset, he has separated us from our sins. He knows us inside and out, keeps in mind that we're made of mud. Men and women don't live very long; like wildflowers they spring up and blossom, But a storm snuffs them out just as quickly, leaving nothing to show they were here. God's love, though, is ever and always, eternally present to all who fear him. O my soul, bless God!

—Psalm 103:10–12, 14–17, 22 (MSG)

God's mercy pours over me. God doesn't give me or you what we deserve for all our sins, all our wrongs. Why? He's a merciful God with immutable mercy.

Instead, He separates me from my sins—not just a couple of feet apart or even a football field apart, where I could still see them on the horizon. No, He has chosen in His mercy to separate my ugly, putrid sins from me as far as the east is from the west and as far as the sunrise is from the sunset.

Why does He choose to separate me from sin and not dangle it in front of my face? One word: love—unconditional, incomprehensible love. "For as high as the heavens are above the earth, so great is His love for those who fear Him" (Psalm 103:11 NIV).

God knows I'm an organic creature with a body, mind, and soul. He knows me inside and out. He made me. And since I'm made of mud, my physical body won't last very long. It will wear out.

Just like on a springtime walk, you notice wildflowers blooming profusely. But when you pass that way again later in the year, you look for the patch of beauty, but it's gone. So it is with us humans; we're here today, gone tomorrow.

But God's love is just the opposite. No matter what season of life I'm in, God's love is present.

Now.
And now.
And now.
This moment.
The next moment and the next.
His love goes on and on eternally; it never stops. It is eternally present to all who fear Him.

> His love goes on and on eternally; it never stops.

That word *fear* is the key. Notice the psalmist said "to all who fear Him." That's because those who fear Him are living in a personal relationship with God and so are able to experience His love—in the present and in the eternally present.

Does God love everyone? Of course. John 3:16 says, "For God so loved the world." But if you are choosing to live away from His love (not fearing Him), it's like you are living on the dark side of the moon. The sun hasn't forsaken the earth, but you never experience its light and warmth.

With God's love, you need to be in a position to receive it. His love is always present, but you're missing out on its benefits since you are choosing to be out of position. You aren't fearing the God who made you, the one who made you to have a love relationship with you—now and forever.

You were made to experience God's love and all the benefits. It's an easy fix. Just change your position.

**Run to the light!
You'll want to stay there and
live in reverential awe of Him.**

Simple. Profound. Life Changing.

> At one time you all had your backs turned to God, thinking rebellious thoughts of him, giving him trouble every chance you got. But now, by giving himself completely at the Cross, actually dying for you, Christ brought you over to God's side and put your lives together, whole and holy in his presence. You don't walk away from a gift like that! You stay grounded and steady in that bond of trust, constantly tuned in to the Message, careful not to be distracted or diverted. There is no other Message—just this one. Every creature under heaven gets this same Message.
>
> —Colossians 1:21–23 (MSG)

Have you ever turned your back on someone? Or has someone done it to you? Or given you that snubbed, I'm-not-going-to-listen-to-you attitude?

Well, that's what we did to God. We are rebellious troublemakers to the King of Kings. Ouch. I mean, who do we think we are?

> You have to accept His gift. It's yours for the taking.

Thankfully, God kept pursuing a love relationship with His creation (us), and Jesus made it all possible by dying on the cross for our putrid, sin-stinking selves.

Jesus brought you over to God's side and put your life together. He's making you whole and holy in His presence. What a gift!

But there's one catch. You have to *want* to accept His gift. It's yours for the taking. This gift is for everyone. But not everyone takes it. That doesn't make sense. We did all the rebelling and troublemaking, and what does He do? He gives us a gift. That behavior doesn't sound so gift worthy to me.

This gift isn't based on your actions. The gift of Jesus, dying for your sin to bring you to God's side, is based on *His* love, character, and desire to have a relationship with His creation—you.

You don't walk away from a gift like that. That would be foolish. Instead, you respond by living a grounded and steady life. Focused. Not allowing yourself to get distracted or diverted from the main thing ...

The message.
The good news.
The gospel.

And what is the gospel? It's the fact that Jesus stepped out of eternity into time for one specific reason: to give us the gift of forgiveness through His death and resurrection so we could live now and for all eternity. All we need to do is believe and accept His life-giving gift.

There is no other message—just this one. This is it.
For you.
For me.
For the world.

Every creature under heaven gets the same message.

So simple.
So profound.
So life changing.

Just Answer the Door

> Every time you cross my mind, I break out in exclamations of thanks to God. There has never been the slightest doubt in my mind that the God who started this great work in you would keep at it and bring it to a flourishing finish on the very day Christ Jesus appears.
>
> —Philippians 1:3, 5–6 (MSG)

What a relationship! A deep, abiding relationship.

Every time this person crossed the apostle Paul's mind, he couldn't help but thank God. Was it this person's friendship, kindness, and generosity that were on display? Those would be great attributes to appreciate of a coworker, but Paul went deeper. He went to the source of those character qualities. He was overwhelmed with thankfulness to God and what God was doing in and through this person. He praised what God was initiating, how God always pursues, and how we need to respond. It's a two-way street.

> He desires a personal relationship with you.

If someone is initiating a relationship with you, the only way you'll benefit from that pursuit is to respond. If not, the relationship is one sided, or it's completely broken off. God, however, never stops pursuing you. He loves you. He desires a personal relationship with you. God wants to start a great work in you. *Not only does He want to start it—He promises to complete it.* There's no unfinished business with God. What He starts He finishes.

Your response to God's love is to respond. Even if you belligerently respond, He will keep pursuing you. He doesn't take no lightly. He doesn't walk away.

He keeps knocking and knocking and knocking. "Here I am! I stand at the door and knock. If anyone hears my voice and opens the door, I will come in and eat with that person, and they with me" (Revelation 3:20 NIV).

Why wouldn't you open the door to the one who desires a life-changing, positive relationship with you?

A relationship that will transform your life into a "great work"?

A relationship with a guarantee of completion and final reward?

Just answer the knock on the door and invite Him in.

Have you allowed God to begin a good work in you? There isn't the slightest doubt in my mind.

**God will keep at you and bring
you to a flourishing finish.**

Right Thinking

The Master said: "These people make a big show of saying the right thing, but their hearts aren't in it. Because they act like they're worshiping me but don't mean it, I'm going to step in and shock them awake, astonish them, stand them on their ears. The wise ones who had it all figured out will be exposed as fools. The smart people who thought they knew everything will turn out to know nothing." Doom to you! You pretend to have the inside track. You shut God out and work behind the scenes, plotting the future as if you knew everything, acting mysterious, never showing your hand. You have everything backward! You treat the potter as a lump of clay. Does a book say to its author, "He didn't write a word of me"? Does a meal say to the woman who cooked it, "She had nothing to do with this"?

—Isaiah 29:13–16 (MSG)

God knows you. God knows everything about you. God knows your heart's motivation. He knows you inside and out. Now for those who know God, this truth brings joy and floods your soul with relief.

However, for those who just pretend to honor God—who make a big show with their lips—God knows that, too. He knows you're a fake. He knows you're putting on a show.

Maybe for your parents.
Maybe for your church.
Maybe for your kids.

But God knows your heart, and He will continue to pursue you so you will become real before Him.

Whatever He needs to do to bring you to Him, He will do, including stepping in and giving you a wake-up call. He knows the most important thing about you is what you think of Him, so He will continue to reveal Himself to you. (One of His names is the self-revealing God.)

Just when you thought you knew it all, having the corner on wisdom, God will expose your foolishness. It is foolish to be acting as if you are God; thinking you have the inside track is a pretend life. (Even then, God's amazing grace is allowing you to shut Him out of your life, living as if He doesn't exist.)

Do you know the future? Do you know whether you'll awaken from your night's sleep? No, only the one who made you and knows you knows!.

> Quit trying to mold God into what *you* want Him to be.

You hope you will awaken in the morning, but only God knows. So put your hope in the one who knows. Then you won't be plotting the future as if you know everything.

He is the Potter. You are the clay.
You are not the Potter. He is not the clay.

Quit trying to mold God into what *you* want Him to be. That is backward thinking and will lead only to God's intervening grace standing you on your ears.

You and I know it would be foolishness, and we would look like fools if we thought the words of a book owned the author. The author owns those words. The author wrote the book. The author shaped those words into his own story. That's what God is doing with you and with me. He is shaping us into His story. He is "preparing" us into the tastiest meal so others "will taste and see that the Lord is good" (Psalm 34:8 NIV).

No more backward thinking.

Chapter 2

Um ... Not So Much

Conviction. Shame. Guilt. More conviction.

The ever-intensifying prayers of my mom were working.

Oswald Chambers was Mom's favorite author. He wrote the classic devotional *My Utmost for His Highest*. In the book Chambers boldly stated that "prayer IS the work."

Mom took this prayer-warrior stuff seriously.

No matter which way I'd turn, somehow my Mom's words, which were peppered with scripture, would haunt me. She would bake my favorite molasses chocolate chip cookies, carefully package them in a roll of paper towels, tuck a handwritten note inside, and mail them to my high-rise dorm at the University of Wisconsin-Oshkosh, where my college coeds would be anxiously awaiting their arrival with me. Sadly, I would grab the unopened card and slip it under my desk pad, not wanting to take a chance at finding some convicting words emanating from it.

However, that note would shout aloud, *Open me!*

It was deafening. I finally had to rip it open just to shut it up—only to find a tenderly written sentiment.

Hey sweetheart! Your favorite cookies come to you with lots of love. Hope you and your roommates enjoy them. Don't miss out on God's best for your life, honey. He loves you so. Me too.

Mom.

Ugh.
So mom-like.
So kind.
So convicting.
But not now. I gotta party.

After five years of college and cookies, I graduated and got married. Just like that.

Graduation one week.

Wedding the next.

Isn't that what I was supposed to do? I was getting not only my BS degree but also my "MRS" degree to a man I thought would rescue me. We had met at a Bible camp years earlier, lost touch, and then reentered each other's lives during my senior year of college. Thinking this was perfect timing, we were each other's saviors—or so we thought.

A huge church wedding ensued, but we had no foundation, and we found ourselves getting divorced in less than two years. Shame and guilt engulfed me. I could hear my precious mom's words ring out. *You're missing out on God's best for you, Margo. He loves you and wants to give you His best. Turn to Him. He's waiting for you.*

Instead of turning to God's best, I turned to the flash and dance of the world, becoming more and more consumed with my image. While I was working at a health club, the manager, a bodybuilder with a huge chest and strong arms, courted me. Thinking I could correct the past mistakes I had made in my first marriage, I married him, unaware that he came with his own unique set of luggage. (Doesn't everyone?)

Our marriage was a roller coaster of emotional, mental, and physical abuse.

We had great times.

He was beautiful to look at, and he knew it. I was just as much the state fair prize on his arm. That's how we dressed, how we looked, and how we acted. We knew we could command the rooms we walked into. Working from ten o'clock in the morning until ten o'clock at night, it was easy to bond with our family of managers and trainers from different gyms. After a twelve-hour day, we'd head out for guacamole and chips at various pubs, staying until closing time. Night after night, we'd laugh together and talk (not always nicely) about all the gym members we had signed up that day. My manager-turned-husband and I thrived at being competitive.

At the beginning of every year, we'd trek to Aspen with good friends, skiing from morning until dusk, until the ski patrols would shoo us off Ajax Mountain. Then by night we'd relax our aching muscles in the hotel's outdoor hot tub as snow softly fell against a moonlit night—only to wake up the next day to do it all over again. It all seemed so idyllic. Somewhat like a Hallmark Christmas movie. Our lives were ones to be envied. We looked the part. We acted the part. We were living the life. Or so I thought.

But there were also horrific times.

I didn't drink, but my health club manager husband did. I never knew whether it was the fifth beer or a shot that would take him over the edge. He'd see someone look at me in a pub, at a baseball game, at a Bucks game, at Summerfest, or just while walking in the mall—and he'd go up to him with his imposing build. "You looking at my wife?" he'd threaten.

Sadly, I knew it was the alcohol talking.

The people with us could usually talk him down or pull him off. Many times I walked home alone or called a cab.

Throughout the years, our gym pals stayed the same even as our careers changed. I ended up in an ad agency, and after one of his blowups, he'd have flowers delivered to me—my favorites, bird-of-paradise. The note always read, "I'm sorry. I love you."

I would give away the flowers to the girls who worked at the agency. They appreciated them way more than I would. I kept the cards though. I don't know why since they just reminded me of all the hurt. At one point, I measured the stack of "I'm sorry" cards: twenty inches high.

> At one point, I measured the stack of "I'm sorry" cards: twenty inches high.

A few more good times were mixed in.

We ran a marathon together. We practiced a lifestyle of nutrition, and he didn't drink while we trained. Plus, I knew I'd be safe with him when running.

And of course my mom would talk to him about Jesus. He'd agree and smirk, feigning respect, but he could never lay his demons down.

Worse times returned.

He once shared with me that anger motivated him. He said he liked to see people grovel. He told me stories, frightening stories, about violent beatings. They were stories to invoke fear. I began to realize that all these stories had occurred while he was under the influence.

He didn't hit me. That wasn't his thing. He was cunning, and broken bones would have been too obvious. I would show up at the agency wearing turtlenecks and scarves, bruises and scratches at my neck. "I have a cat," I told my coworkers. (I wasn't fooling anyone.) I covered the hand prints from the attempted choking.

It was always alcohol that started the raging. We'd be out and having fun; somebody would look at me, and he would get into people's faces and explosively impose himself before them. I would walk away.

And all the while, my mom kept praying for me as she kept trusting the unseen. She had no idea about my abusive marriage since I hid it quite well; I didn't want to be another failure to myself or my family. She knew something was amiss but also knew God was at work, and she wasn't about to give up now.

Decent moments returned.

We traveled the United States and most of Canada with his souped-up El Dorado Cadillac, complete with funky wheels and a horn that blared, "Yes, Sir, That's My Baby." Along our journey, we met people in health clubs across the country, especially falling in love with the Chicago health club scene. We had a blast. My faithful dog, Joplin, a German shepherd/husky accompanied us. She hung her head out that big Cadillac window, making passersby smile.

However, the best time of all was when my husband decided on his own that he wasn't going to drink anymore. He rid our entire home of all the liquor and beer, and for about six weeks, maybe even a couple of months, I had a whole new husband, a whole new marriage. I thought we'd really made it. In the middle of this new bliss, I went out with some girlfriends after work to Chi-Chi's and had "guac" (of course) and chips. I remember telling them, "I need to be home by ten thirty because my husband will be home by then."

I was living in hope. They looked at me, wanting to believe but unbelieving. I made sure to be home on time. I waited for my new, sober husband. Then it was eleven o'clock, eleven thirty, midnight ...

That's when the worst time came.

He had gone to a bachelor party, and my coworker was at that same party. I don't remember how late it was when the coworker called.

He said, "Margo, your husband has done horrific things here. He's drunker than I've ever seen him." It was the kind of scene you'd picture for a bachelor party. "I have him," he said, "in my car. My wife is with me. He fell down and broke his glasses."

I said, "Oh, he doesn't need them. They're just vanity glasses." (He was always up on the latest trends.)

"Margo, that's not all," my friend continued. "He has a gun, and he's going to come kill you. He's been telling people about it all night."

My husband had passed out. He had done cocaine that night, and I never even knew it was one of his vices. "We're going to take him home because I know he's going to come kill you. You need to leave … tonight. You need to get out."

My coworker and his wife were angels to me. They took him, armed and high, into their home, laying him on the couch and putting themselves at risk to buy me time to escape. I had a bicycle and a backpack, and I left. I hid with a girlfriend, who was eight months pregnant, and her husband. I kept my job, so eventually my husband knew where I was. I knew I was being watched. In return, I put a restraining order on him, but those things are about as good as the paper they're written on.

When you finally share something about being in an abusive relationship, you have built so much shame in yourself over the fact that you know you're living a double life that you think others will look at you that way, too. You blame yourself. That's why abused women don't leave. It's their fault. They can fix it.

God just extracted him from my life. He moved to California. I never knew I was his fifth wife.

And my mom prayed on.

Mom told me years later that she'd had no idea I would have to hit lower than rock bottom before I would look up.

"Oh honey, I'm just so grateful that you're alive," she exclaimed.

There was no blame.

She "knew that she knew" God was able. I can still hear her quoting Ephesians 3:20 (NIV). "Now to Him who is able to do immeasurably more than all we ask or imagine, according to His power that is at work within us."

Once again, this woman wouldn't be moved. She firmly stood on God's promises.

The minute I was out the door of our fashionable eastside condo, when I ran from him that night, my thoughts raced. How had I gotten to this point in my life? I was from a wonderful, God-fearing home with a mom and dad who loved and cared for me. I had two amazing older sisters. I had been an honor student, a band and orchestra student and a pom-pom girl; I had tons of friends. I was a college graduate and my company's vice president. How had I gotten down to having only a backpack of clothes, my bicycle, and my bigger-than-Mary Poppins purse as I left in my Mazda RX-7 in the dark of night?

There was no time to think, only time to react to the situation. As I closed the front door behind me, I knew my life would change forever. Would I finally heed this wake-up call?

Things looked pretty bleak.

In the last years of my ex-husband's life, his daughter and her husband, a pastor, became instrumental in his life. He even began listening to the Bible on audio. He ultimately died from the physical toll of alcohol, but he came to know Jesus first. Hallelujah! (How do I know this? Gratefully, his two adult daughters found me through social media to tell me about their dad and to regain contact with each other after many, many years of being apart.)

> I looked at him through the compassionate eyes of Jesus.

Just think, after all those subsequent years of praying for him (and of course Mom continued to pray for him) to come to know Jesus—and now, I'll know the real him one day. I looked at him through the compassionate eyes of Jesus, like Jesus looked at me, and I forgave him.

Completely.

Fully.

You know you've truly forgiven someone when you want to bless that person. You want the best for him or her. And that's just what I did. I even asked him to please forgive me for the numerous times my cutting words had hurt him—to the point of provoking his anger. Until that moment came, though, I had other trials to overcome.

My dad died suddenly in his sleep. We were supposed to go to our annual Wisconsin Badger football game, and instead he moved to heaven. The ad agency I was climbing up in went bankrupt, and my second divorce began—all within the same year. I plodded on. After all, I prided myself in being a survivor. I filled my life with dating professional basketball and hockey players.

And my mom prayed on.

Mom knew that, when we pray, God works; and when we work, we work. So mom kept at the work of intercession. She wasn't about to stop now. In fact, she called her fellow prayer warriors—Barb, Gloria, Kathryn, Katherine, and Grandma Lanz—to ramp up their petitions to the throne.

God was working behind the scenes.

My hardened heart was beginning to crack.

My theme song of "I Got This" was fading into "Um … Not So Much."

Why is it, Lord, that I don't want to listen to Your whispers? Instead, it's in the trials that I begin to hear You. I start to feel Your loving, eternal thumb pressure bearing down on me.

I hear You but still shut You out. Nevertheless, You continue to lovingly pursue me and heap burning coals on my head of conviction.

Help me to see conviction as a good thing, not something to try to run from. Forgive me for excusing my actions and placing blame on everyone else.

You want me to turn to You, repent of my sinful ways, and receive Your best, as Mom always said. I see now that Mom was always right.

Devotions
for Your Next Right Steps

Conviction

Search and Rescue
Running in the Right Direction
Holds My Life Together
Adventurously Expectant Life
Passing the Ultimate Test
God's Free Gift

Search and Rescue

> The heart is hopelessly dark and deceitful, a puzzle that no one can figure out. But I, God, search the heart and examine the mind. I get to the heart of the human. I get to the root of things. I treat them as they really are, not as they pretend to be.
>
> —Jeremiah 17:9–10 (MSG)

Aren't you glad God can get to the root of things? That means He digs deep. He has to be able to get past all the dirt and expose the root.

He can see through your exterior, your facade, right into your heart and mind. And that's a very good thing, since the prophet Jeremiah tells us, "The heart is hopelessly dark and deceitful, a puzzle no one can figure out."

But God can, He gets to the human heart, mind, will, and emotions. And thank You, God. You can and do see through our exterior, since no one else is able to change the human heart but You.

> He gets to the human heart, mind, will, and emotions.

We would be hopelessly dark and deceitful without God initiating the search and rescue of our hearts and minds. He sees through all the pretenses. He already knows the solution to the puzzle.

So when you pretend to be "right" with God, God, who has already searched your heart and mind, treats you as you really are—no matter how much you pretend to be okay. You're trying to convince yourself that your heart and mind are basically good.

But the acceptance that your heart is hopelessly dark and deceitful, and that *only God can get to the heart of a human, specifically your heart*, is victory. Only then can God go to work—digging deep and revealing the wickedness and deceit in your heart.

No more rationalizing.
No more pretending.
He changes the darkness into light.

Running in the Right Direction

> The people I love, I call to account—prod and correct and guide so that they'll live at their best. Up on your feet, then! About face! Run after God!
>
> —Revelation 3:19 (MSG)

A prodding God. He cares enough to urge, exhort, motivate, provoke, and stimulate me to live at my best.

He wants me to live—really live. And He knows what it takes to rouse me. Not to settle.

His great love for me compels Him to prod. Just like a parent exhibits to a precious child, He calls me to account for my actions, but thankfully He doesn't leave me there. He prods when necessary, corrects when wrong, and guides my missteps.

What love! He is continually honing me. That's a lot of work.

Prod. Correct. Guide.

Prod. Correct. Guide.

Until you and I are shaped into the likeness of Him. Then I can live at my very best.

He never gives up. He never quits on me. His desire is to have me turn around and run after Him. No running away from Him anymore.

> As He guides me, I am changed.

And how does He accomplish this about-face in me? It is mainly through His Word. It's the only book that reads you as you read it.

Conviction. Response. Change.
Conviction. Response. Change.

So as He prods me, there is conviction. As He corrects me, I respond. And as He guides me, I'm changed. My missteps become His unwavering steps.

I'm now living at my best. I have turned around (repented of my ways).

I'm on my feet and at the ready to respond to His every prod, correction, and guidance.

It's a grateful way of life. I want His intimate care, His amazing love. I desire to stay accountable to Him. That pursuit keeps me at my best and keeps me running after God.

So when I feel His prod, I know that I know He loves me and is calling me higher. My conviction turns into a response, and I'm able to see a change of heart.

**I am now living at my best,
which is His best for me.**

Holds My Life Together

> We look at this Son (Jesus) and see the God who cannot be seen. We look at this Son and see God's original purpose in everything created. For everything, absolutely everything, above and below, visible and invisible, rank after rank after rank of angels—everything got started in Him and finds its purpose in Him. He was there before any of it came into existence and holds it all together right up to this moment.
>
> —Colossians 1:15–17 (MSG)

What is your purpose in life? What are your goals? Is it acquiring more and more stuff? Or planning more and more outings? Then you'll need to be earning more and more money. The list could go on and on. When is the "more and more" going to be enough? When will you be satiated?

The apostle Paul shares that "everything got started in Jesus, God's Son, and everything finds its purpose in Him." So your real purpose—that nagging void inside you—is drawing you to be filled with Jesus, to finally be satiated, to be satisfied completely. Only Jesus can satisfy you to overflowing, since "everything finds its purpose in Him."

That includes absolutely everything. And everything is every thing, including everything above and below. Everything visible and invisible. Every angel. Everything created. That includes me. That includes you.

So if you're existing to accumulate wealth, stuff, fame, honor roll kids, and temporary fixes of happiness, those will soon fade from view. (No permanent satiation there.) Turn to the one who was "there before any of it came into existence and holds it all together right up to this moment."

And since we can hold onto only this moment, since we don't know about the next, why live to accumulate the stuff that doesn't last?

**Live a purpose-filled life,
one only Jesus can provide.**

Adventurously Expectant Life

> So don't you see that we don't owe this old do-it-yourself life one red cent. There's nothing in it for us, nothing at all. The best thing to do is give it a decent burial and get on with your new life. God's Spirit beckons. There are things to do and places to go! This resurrection life you received from God is not a timid, grave-tending life. It's adventurously expectant, greeting God with a childlike "What's next, Papa?" God's Spirit touches our spirits and confirms who we really are. We know who He is, and we know who we are: Father and children. And we know we are going to get what's coming to us—an unbelievable inheritance!
>
> —Romans 8:12–16 (MSG)

I used to believe that if I followed Jesus with all my heart, soul, mind, and strength that I would be destined for "Dullsville." I'd need to wear my hair in a bun, don a long jean skirt, sans makeup, and head for the great unknown in Africa somewhere.

Wow! Was I wrong! There are those who are called to that type of service, and God calls others to the service that meets their personal passions. The trying-to-do-your-own-thing life is arduous, lackluster; and it has no long-term payoff. In fact, the apostle Paul stated that "there's nothing in it for us, nothing at all."

The new, powerful resurrection life through the Spirit of God living in me is full of the kind of adventure that fulfills me—full of purpose, full of relationship. Father to a child.

Knowing that Daddy's got this as I confidently hold His hand, walking through this great adventure called life.

And wherever He takes me, I know if I keep holding onto His hand, I'll be just fine. More than fine actually.

I'll be protected.
Counseled.
Encouraged.
Hugged.
Convicted.
Assured.

> Wherever He takes me, I know that if I keep holding onto His hand, I'll be just fine.

He really knows me, and I know Him. I am in His forever family with a forever home.

So when God's Spirit beckons, I respond. No doubts. No fear. No asking why. No debate. Just confidence in knowing He has the best things for me to do and the best places for me to go.

I don't need to know how my adventure is going to play out. He knows, and that's more than good enough for me as I hold tightly to His hand, expectantly asking, "What's next, Papa?"

He smiles at me, and we walk on.

Passing the Ultimate Test

> Here's how you test for the genuine Spirit of God. Everyone who confesses openly his faith in Jesus Christ—the Son of God, who came as an actual flesh-and-blood person—comes from God and belongs to God. And everyone who refuses to confess faith in Jesus has nothing in common with God.
>
> —1 John 4:2–3 (MSG)

Straightforward words. No beating around the bush. This verse dispels the popular notion that there are many ways up the mountain. Uh, no, there aren't. There is only one way to Father God, and that is through His Son, Jesus Christ. "I am the way, the truth and the life. No one comes to the Father, but by me." (That's Jesus speaking in John 14:6.)

You can even test and see whether you have the genuine Spirit of God. Simply stated. Easy to do. Here it is—if you confess openly your faith in Jesus Christ, the Son of God, then you are in God's family. You belong to God. Woo-hoo!

Conversely, the opposite is true. If you do not confess openly by faith in Jesus Christ, the Son of God, then you are not in God's family. You don't belong to God. In fact, you have nothing in common with Him.

God makes it so easy to be part of His family. Why do we make it so hard? He desires for you to belong to the greatest family—His—but you decide, "No thanks, I'm good."

God has made a simple way for you, but that way cost everything for His Son. This Jesus, who stepped out of eternity into time and came as an actual flesh-and-blood person, came to die for all your yuck (sin). You couldn't possibly have paid for that enormous debt you incurred. Only Jesus could do that. And he did! "No one can take my life from me. I sacrifice it voluntarily. For I have the authority to lay it down when I want to and also to take it up again. For this is what my Father has commanded" (Jesus speaking in John 10:18).

> God has made a simple way for you, but that way cost everything for His Son.

So Jesus willingly went to the cross for you, was resurrected from the dead for you, and is seated at the right hand of God. He is ever interceding right this moment for you so you could *live* by His Spirit and belong to God forever. What a deal! He did it all. He's yours for the taking.

However, it's only by openly confessing your faith in Jesus that cements the deal. No sneaking into God's family.

Confessing means "calling it the same thing as." So when you are openly confessing your faith in Jesus Christ, there is no confusion between you and Father God. He sees your heart. He hears your open confession of faith in His Son.

You are in.

You belong to God.

Just think … He did it *all* for you. All you need to do is confess and believe.

Why wouldn't you want to belong to the best family in the whole world? Plus, you get to be together for all eternity. (That's a very long time.) No abandonment issues here. You are in God's forever family through Jesus, His Son.

So administer your own test. Do you have the genuine Spirit of God living in you?

He doesn't want you to fail.

God's Free Gift

Now God has us where he wants us, with all the time in this world and the next to shower grace and kindness upon us in Christ Jesus. Saving is all his idea, and all his work. All we do is trust him enough to let him do it. It's God's gift from start to finish! We don't play the major role. If we did, we'd probably go around bragging that we'd done the whole thing! No, we neither make nor save ourselves. God does both the making and saving. He creates each of us by Christ Jesus to join him in the work he does, the good work he has gotten ready for us to do, work we had better be doing.

—Ephesians 2:7–10 (MSG)

Run to God and stay right there. He has such wonderful plans for you. And He has you where He wants you—with all the time in this world and the next. (He's the Creator of time, so there's no need to worry about this time on earth or for all eternity. It's safe in His hands.)

And you know what He wants to do with you? Shower grace and kindness on you in Jesus. Why would you want to run anywhere else other than to His loving arms? Who doesn't want grace and kindness showered over him or her?

All you need to do is trust. Yep, that's it. Trust Him enough to let Him save you. He does all the work. You do all the trusting. Salvation is His gift to you.

What do you do with a gift? Scrutinize it? Examine the type of wrapping paper and size of box it's in before you decide to open it? Of course not. That would be ludicrous. You graciously accept the gift. Open and enjoy it.

God's free gift to us is this: salvation through His Son, Jesus. He died so we could be forgiven of our sin, which separates us from God. Jesus has done it all—signed, sealed, and delivered. The gift is yours for the taking.

Saving you is all God's idea. It's His gift to you. You cannot make or save yourself. And if you try, you will make a mess of your life.

> God's free gift to us is this: salvation through His Son, Jesus.

So run to God.

Join Him in what He had planned for you from the very beginning. And what's that? To live a purpose-filled life. To join Jesus in doing good works. To be like Him. To make a difference in your sphere of influence. "God created you in Christ Jesus to join him in the work he does, the good work he has gotten us ready for us to do. Work we had better be doing!"

Run to Him and accept His gift, the free gift of salvation.

He offers His gift to everyone.

Chapter 3

What Took You So Long?

"I've been waiting for you."
"Once I was blind, but now I see."
That was it.
A revelation.
An epiphany.

Just like Jesus miraculously healed the man who was born blind in chapter 9 of the book of John, Jesus cured my blindness. God didn't give me just any cure. It was the perfect cure. It was sight—not physical sight but spiritual sight, the ultimate sight.

All it took was believing Jesus was who He said He was. It's true. It's not only true in the general sense but true for *me*.

The blind man told the Pharisees that this "Jesus" person healed him on the Sabbath. This deed was taboo, according to the religious zealots. When the Pharisees harassed the man about Jesus, he responded, "One thing I do know. I was blind, but now I see."

I came to know Jesus just like the blind man did. Actually, that's how we all come to accept Jesus as our personal Savior, Healer, and Friend. Let's look at the rest of the story from John 9:35–38 (NIV). "Jesus heard that they had thrown him out, and when He found him, He said, 'Do you believe in the Son of Man?' 'Who is he, sir?' the man asked. 'Tell me so that I may believe in him.' Jesus said, 'You have now seen him; in fact, he is the one speaking with you.' Then the man said, 'Lord, I believe,' and he worshiped him."

Once I believed, too, the eyes of my heart saw the truth. His name is Jesus. Jesus said in John 14:6, "I am the way, the truth and the life. No one comes to the Father, but by me."

He is the cure. He doesn't give you some holy medicine or a super bandage to try to patch up your old self. He gives you Himself. You are made new.

I remember meeting Jesus on a gloriously sunny summer day in a small-town square in Wisconsin. The occasion was my sister's company picnic.

I knew all about Jesus.

I knew the Bible stories.

I could quote the scriptures.

I knew all the rhyme and memory rituals, but they were just head knowledge.

I tried to banter Him away, but the more I wanted to be right in my own eyes, the more my mom would pray. (Of course she did.) It was evident she was entreating God Almighty to show Himself to me, since she knew one of His names as the self-revealing God. Continual stop signs would pop up in my life, as if God Himself were calling out to me. "Here I am, Margo." It seemed at every turn I would bump into Him. At times, I felt like He was playing hide-and-seek with a two-year-old. While playing that childhood

> The more I wanted to be right in my own eyes, the more my mom would pray.

game, you wouldn't hole up in the basement so the toddler had no chance of finding you. No, you'd allow yourself to be revealed by every so often calling out to the running-the-wrong-way youngster. That's exactly what the Hound of Heaven, Jesus, did with me, except every time He revealed Himself, I ran from Him, not to Him.

After all, my security came from my image, relationships, career, health, and wealth. Those were false securities. I was secure in my false securities. But thankfully, God knew me more than I knew myself and never stopped pursuing me in all His loving-kindness, just like He will never stop pursuing you.

It was a total revelation from the personal, seeking-a-relationship-with-me God when I went from blind to sight on that swing set on that cloudless day in that American town.

I felt like how the blind man must have felt when the Pharisees were questioning him, and he kept boldly stating, "All I know is once I was blind and now I see."

It was revelation.

No, I didn't actually see His face, but I knew Jesus was there. After all, He had been pursuing me ever since I was little. This time, however, my heart rejoiced that He would still want to initiate a relationship with me after all I had done. I was drawn to Him. I didn't want to escape His love, grace (undeserved favor), or mercy (not getting what I deserved) anymore.

My "I got this" attitude had morphed into a less certain "Um ...not so much." Now Jesus was standing at the door of my heart and knocking.

I wanted to let Him in.

Jesus said in Revelation 3:20, "Here I am! I stand at the door and knock. If anyone hears my voice and opens the door, I will come in and eat with that person, and they with me." He never breaks down the door to have a relationship with you. He just stands patiently at the door, continually knocking until you open it. What a gentleman! Jesus waited all those years for me to answer the door.

I vividly remember a classic painting, depicting the Revelation 3:20 verse, that hung in the bedroom hallway of my childhood home. I couldn't help but pass by it numerous times a day. I was transfixed by the figure of Jesus, who stood at an arched door, knocking. Plus, I noted a uniqueness about that door; it had no door handle, so no one was able to open it from the outside. There was no way Jesus could have entered the doorway unless the person inside opened it and invited Him in.

That's just what I finally did.

It didn't look like that idyllic painting, but I remember inviting Jesus to enter through the door of my life. Hanging upside down on the swinging trapeze bar while Mom was still soaring on the swing, I jumped off and jubilantly exclaimed, "I'm not going to live for myself anymore, Mom. I'm not going to sow to my flesh. I'm going to live for Jesus all the rest of my days."

> He had already forgiven my past, present, and future sin.

What had just emerged from my mouth? It erupted from my overflowing heart. I had decided to follow Jesus. There was no turning back. I recognized and owned my own yuck, my own sin. I owned what Jesus had died for on the cross. He had already forgiven my past, present, and future sin. It was *my* sin that had put Him on the cross. He didn't even need your sin. Mine was enough to keep Him there.

Romans 3:23–25 says, "For all have sinned and fall short of the glory of God, and ALL are justified freely by His grace through the redemption that came through Christ Jesus. God presented Christ as a sacrifice of atonement, through the shedding of His blood—to be received by faith."

By faith, I confessed my sin and repented. In other words, I finally admitted that my wrongs were sin. I quit blaming everyone else for my putrid behavior. I had excused my poor conduct long enough. I came to the end of my sin and did a complete 180-degree turn around. I wasn't running to sin anymore. I was running to God. I had a change of heart and mind. I was determined to avoid such behaviors in the future by daily yielding to Him in unwavering faith.

I wasn't sure what repenting would entail, but it didn't matter anymore. Jesus had captured my heart, and I desired to know Him more and more. To do that, confessing and repenting were the steps I needed to take.

Mom hurriedly jumped off the swing and threw her arms up into the bluer-than-blue sky, exclaiming, "Hallelujah!" (the highest form of praise). "Thank You, Jesus," she cried out as tears of joy ran from her dark-brown, doe-like eyes.

Just like the woman at the well, we speedily went to find my sister and her friends to tell them that Jesus, the Hound of Heaven, had become my personal Savior. (And, by the way, He wants to be yours, too.)

After all those years of running from Jesus, when I finally fell into His arms, He kindly whispered in my ear, "What took you so long? I've been waiting for you."

Thank You, Jesus, for making me a new creation. You just didn't temporarily patch the holes in my exterior but sacrificed Your perfect and holy life for my sinful, putrid life so I could become holy and whole in You. My old self is gone, and I've become brand new. I am humbled by Your complete forgiveness of all my sin—past, present, and future. Please help me to keep right in the middle of the road You have marked out for me. I'm excited to walk in the best plans You have for me. I don't want any more detours. I want steps that are unwaveringly next to You.

Devotions
for Your Next Right Steps

No More Detours Away from the Heart of God

Bragging Rights Forever
Always within Earshot
My Heart, Christ's Home
Bring Out the Best in You
WWJS: What Would Jesus Say?

Bragging Rights Forever

> For my part, I am going to boast about nothing but the Cross of our Master, Jesus Christ. Because of that Cross, I have been crucified in relation to the world, set free from the stifling atmosphere of pleasing others and fitting into the little patterns that they dictate. Can't you see the central issue in all this? It is not what you and I do ... It is what God is doing, and he is creating something totally new, a free life!
>
> —Galatians 6:14–15 (MSG)

What do you boast about? Does your car sport a bumper sticker that says, "My child is an honor student"? Do you have a huge mounted muskie donning the wall of your home office? On your refrigerator, is there a framed "treasure" from your three-year-old?

It's natural to boast of one's accomplishments. It's not always done in a prideful way but in such a way that honors an amazing job.

Here, the apostle Paul wants to boast of only one thing: Jesus's accomplishment on the cross.

The cross blew Paul away. The cross made a huge difference in his life. The cross of Jesus humbled him. The cross of Master Jesus rescued him forever. How could he not boast?

The cross isn't just one of the many things he boasted about. It was the only thing.

Do you have one thing you boast about? Is it the saving work of Jesus on the cross for you? Without the cross, you would be lost, but now you are found. That's something to boast about.

Paul had been blaspheming this same Jesus for years until he saw the light—literally. In the midst of Paul's wayward actions and misguided thinking, Jesus stepped into his life to save him (just like He does with us). Jesus saved Paul from "the stifling atmosphere of pleasing others and fitting into the little patterns they dictate."

That's a big deal.

God is creating something totally new—a free life. No more answering to everyone around you. Only Jesus! He provided you with a way out by His cross. Not only do you live above the fray now, but the cross comes with a guarantee that you are free in this life—and the next.

> God is creating something totally new . . . a free life.

You are forever free because of Jesus's accomplishment.

No wonder Paul wanted to boast about only one thing.

The cross intersected his life,
    stopped him in his tracks,
        and brought him to his repentant knees.

When he deserved death, the cross breathed life into his very soul. Have you been there? Have you been to the cross of Christ? Are you staying there and boasting of Jesus's accomplishment?

The cross far outweighs anything anyone has ever accomplished.

Always within Earshot

> This is God's Message, the God who made earth, made it livable and lasting, known everywhere as God: "Call to me and I will answer you. I'll tell you marvelous and wondrous things that you could never figure out on your own."
>
> —Jeremiah 33:2–3 (MSG)

Have you ever called to a person and gotten no response? Maybe you called across a room to your friend—or perhaps to your daughter, who was playing with the dog. Or to your son, who was doing his homework.

No answer.

Not even a nod.

Maybe the person you called was deep in thought. Maybe he or she was actively engaged in what he or she was doing. Maybe the person heard but just chose to ignore your voice. You called but got no answer.

Don't fret. There is one who will always hear your call. Always. And not only will He hear your voice, He will answer you. You won't just get polite recognition of "I heard you," but you'll get a response to your exact call.

> There is one who will always hear your call. Always.

Jesus never chooses to look away. He never pretends you didn't call. He is thrilled that you chose to call

Him. He is at the ready to answer you and "tell you marvelous and wondrous things that you could never figure out on your own."

Now that's the person to always call. That's the person to have first on your smartphone "Favorites." That's the person to totally rely on. God wants you to call to Him.

Call to Him.
In everything.
Every situation.
Every decision.
Every detail.
Nothing is too big or too small.
Just call.

Remember God's promise: He will always answer. And that's a promise with dividends. Not only does He answer, but He will tell you the "inside scoop." His marvelous and wondrous ways are yours for the taking.

The one who always answers is God, who made the earth. He made it livable. He made it lasting. He is known everywhere as God. He comes with impressive credentials. He is at your disposal just for the calling.

And why wouldn't you want to call a person who desires to respond to your personal call?

Call out to Jesus.
He promises to listen.
He promises to answer.
He is always within earshot.

Will you listen to His personal answer?

My Heart, Christ's Home

> But if God himself has taken up residence in your life, you can hardly be thinking more of yourself than of him. Anyone, of course, who has not welcomed this invisible but clearly present God, the Spirit of Christ, won't know what we're talking about. But for you who welcome him, in whom he dwells—even though you still experience all the limitations of sin—you yourself experience life on God's terms. When God lives and breathes in you (and he does, as surely as he did in Jesus), you are delivered from that dead life. With his Spirit living in you, your body will be as alive as Christ's!
>
> —Romans 8:9, 11 (MSG)

Have you heard the phrase "living above the line"? It's exactly what Paul was talking about in Romans 8. You are experiencing life on God's terms now. You aren't living the low life, the dead life. You are alive and filled up to overflowing with the Spirit of Christ or the Holy Spirit.

God Himself has taken up residency in you. He lives *in* you. In other words, the same power that raised Jesus from the dead lives in you—that's some power. That's why you are able to "live above the line."

Once you were dead in your sin (the low life). A sinful life is the life that puts *I* on the throne. (Remember, sin is spelled s-I-n. Notice the big *I* in the middle.)

Then you "welcomed this invisible, yet clearly present God, the Spirit of Christ" to come in and invade your life. So now you are already delivered from "that dead life." That's the life of pursuing your wants, your ways, and your rights. However, with God's "Spirit living in you, your body will be as alive as Christ's."

That is an amazing thought to comprehend, to steep in. It's incredible to know that when I accept Him by faith, He gladly comes in, makes His home in me, and starts cleaning every bedroom, garage, basement, and closet of my life.

Before He can go to work in me, I need to give Him permission. And when I do, watch out! The greatest ongoing transformation takes place. My heart becomes Christ's home. Now He not only has cleaned up my rooms, but I have given Him the deed to my home. He now owns every part of me.

The Holy Spirit dwells in me. He lives and breathes in me so I can experience life to the full. It's the life He always meant for me. It's the life that lives above the line. It's a powerful life. No more being dragged down by the weight of low living. No more being dragged down by the weight of sin.

> No more being dragged down by the weight of low living.

I am forgiven.
I am free.
I can fly.

Bring Out the Best in You

You're familiar with the old written law, "Love your friend," and its unwritten companion, "Hate your enemy." I'm challenging that. I'm telling you to love your enemies. Let them bring out the best in you, not the worst. When someone gives you a hard time, respond with the energies of prayer, for then you are working out of your true selves, your God-created selves. This is what God does: He gives his best—the sun to warm and the rain to nourish—to everyone, regardless: the good and bad, the nice and nasty. If all you do is love the lovable, do you expect a bonus? Anybody can do that. If you simply say hello to those who greet you, do you expect a medal? Any run-of-the-mill sinner does that. In a word, what I'm saying is, Grow up. You're kingdom subjects. Now live like it. Live out your God-created identity. Live generously and graciously toward others, the way God lives toward you.

—Matthew 5:43–48 (MSG)

"Grow up." I've heard those words before. From my parents. From a teacher. From my mentor. From some friends. These words were usually said in exasperation, since I was probably acting way beneath my chronological age.

However, in the verses from Matthew 5 above, Jesus Himself admonished in His ever-perfect concern for me to "grow up." He sees how easy it is for me to love my friends but hate my enemies.

But that isn't His way. That way certainly doesn't show His kingdom is in me and is my pursuit. So, of course, His desire is to challenge me with truth. (After all, He is the truth, so it would be fitting to respond rightly.)

Jesus wants me to love my enemies. Really? My first reaction is, "You've got to be kidding, Jesus!" However, my thoughtful reaction knows He has a grander purpose for me, His purpose.

God doesn't want my selfish ways but His selfless ways. God desires to bring out the best in me, which doesn't include wallowing in my worst.

I must act rightly when I am wronged. That's what Jesus did. He ran to His Father and told Him all about His enemies—not to condemn them but to help them. Jesus prayed for them. He didn't just pray a popcorn-type prayer—a one-liner that shoots up to heaven in quick desperation. No, Jesus prayed a purposeful, life-changing prayer that required energy. Required time. Required faith, knowing that His Father hears and will respond in His time and way.

> I must act rightly when I am wronged.

And as I pray, God works. He does surgery not only on my enemies' hearts but most importantly on mine. I become more and more like Him and less and less like my putrid self.

And since He gives His best, He expects me to give my best, which is actually His best in me.

Love the unlovable. Only He can do that through me.

Be friendly to the unfriendly. Only He can do that through me.

Pray for the putrid. Only He can do that through me.

That's why God encourages me, exhorts me, to "grow up!" Don't just live my run-of-the-mill sinful ways. I am a kingdom subject. Live like it. Live out my God-created identity. Not my "Margo identity." Not your (your name here) identity.

My focus should be on King Jesus. After all, I am His subject, and that identity frees me to live generously and graciously. Yes, even with my enemies. And living God's way, they won't stay my enemies for long. After all, that's how He lives toward me—generously and graciously.

**Live God's way
generously and graciously toward others.**

WWJS: What Would Jesus Say?

> Though some tongues just love the taste of gossip, those who follow Jesus have better uses for language than that. Don't talk dirty or silly. That kind of talk doesn't fit our style. Thanksgiving is our dialect.
>
> —Ephesians 5:4 (MSG)

As a follower of Jesus, your dialect should be the language Jesus would use. And that dialect flows out of a grateful heart. Your speech should be full of thanksgiving, which will stand out from standard language. It shouldn't contain dirty talk, silly talk, or gossip.

Juicy morsels of gossip can wait on your tongue at the ready to be blurted out at just the right time to just the right person. Since you want to please Jesus, you have way better uses for your words than gossiping.

Your tongue is intended to edify and build one another up, not to cut down and destroy. Dirty talk is to have no welcome in your dialect. Coarse joking and sarcasm cut down others. Period. It's easy to hide, or think we're hiding, the put-downs by adding remarks such as "Oh, I was only kidding" or "Come on, don't be so sensitive.". The apostle Paul instructed us to know that kind of talk doesn't fit our style. It's not Jesus's style.

And what is Jesus's style? He told us a few verses before in Ephesians.

My assumption is that you have paid careful attention to Christ, been well instructed in the truth precisely as we have it in Jesus. Since, then, we do not have the excuse of ignorance, everything—and I do mean everything—connected with that old way of life has to go. It's rotten through and through. Get rid of it! And then take on an entirely new way of life—a God-fashioned life, a life renewed from the inside and working itself into your conduct as God accurately reproduces his character in you. Watch the way you talk. Let nothing foul or dirty come out of your mouth. Say only what helps, each word a gift. Don't grieve God. Don't break his heart. His Holy Spirit, moving and breathing in you, is the most intimate part of your life, making you fit for himself. Don't take such a gift for granted. Make a clean break with all cutting, backbiting, profane talk. Be gentle with one another, sensitive. Forgive one another as quickly and thoroughly as God in Christ forgave you.

(Ephesians 4:20–24, 29–32 MSG)

Jesus's direction is pretty straightforward. The old way of life has got to go, which includes the old "standard language," since you have taken on a completely new way of life—a God-fashioned life. That means your new dialect says only what helps.

> Your new dialect says only what helps.

Each word is a gift.

Chapter 4

Squeegee the Shower

How I learned to do the next right thing.
 Grace.
 Grace upon grace.
 Grace upon grace upon grace.
 As a speaker and Bible teacher, I've had the opportunity to share my story and its lessons from many a platform. Often when I present, a precious friend of mine joins me, since she has an amazing gift for worship music. She usually closes the session with

> His grace is without pause—without end.

> But for Your grace, I'd not be saved.
> But for Your grace, I'd go my way.
> I'm forever grateful, that You have been faithful to me,
> Lord, for Your amazing grace ...
> I once was lost but now I'm found, was blind but now I see.

God can be nothing but gracious. His grace is without pause—without end. He is abounding in grace. When all is said and done, we will still be standing in His grace. I love grace. I need grace. I want His undeserved favor poured over me. That's just what God allowed with my third marriage—this time to a man who follows hard after Jesus (although that wasn't always the case).

Just six months after my "swing-set epiphany," I was on a photo shoot assignment when I stopped at a hotel's row of pay phones to call for my messages at the ad agency. (Yes, this was before cell phones had arrived on the scene.) Although I was unaware of it at the time, the guy to my left had been calling back to his office while somewhat listening to my conversations. He was trying to time the moment perfectly to be able to hand me his business card and ask me to lunch. I hung up the receiver and scurried out of sight into the frigid winter weather, much to my suitor's chagrin. Fortunately for him (and me), "nature called," and back inside I dashed, only for said suitor to approach me in the vestibule.

To this day, his words are etched in my memory. "Excuse me. Would you like to do lunch with me sometime?"

I searched for how to respond, since six months before I had committed my life to Jesus, and I wasn't about to be tripped up now.

So as he stood with business card in outstretched hand, I blurted, "No thanks. I'm working right now. Plus, I used to be picked up in health clubs and bars, but now I have decided to follow Jesus."

He responded, "Oh, I'm sorry. I didn't mean to bother you."

Thinking I had been a bit curt, I apologized, and we did the obligatory business card exchange. Off I went, back into the cold, never to see that mysterious man in the tan trench coat ever again—or so I thought.

I have heard it said that "when you want to make God laugh, tell Him your plans." Or, as the Bible puts it in Proverbs 16:9, "In their hearts humans plan their course, but the Lord establishes their steps." Well, I may have walked out in the cold, *but God* had plans to bring great warmth into my life as I continued to follow Him step-by-step. Eventually, those steps led me right back to the man who'd originally stalked me at a pay phone.

From that divine meeting at a row of pay phones to his coming to know Jesus, my unknown suitor was now the man God had chosen for me—not in the way I would have chosen, however. Brian continued to actively pursue me, even though I painstakingly told him about my sordid past. Any other man would have run in the opposite direction; instead Brian ran *to* me. Within six months and two life-changing dates—to a Josh McDowell (a Christian apologist) seminar and a Dave Roever (an inspirational speaker and author) concert—Brian put his trust in the Lord Jesus Christ. Three years later we were married on the idyllic island of Maui.

Throughout our early years of marriage, God continued to nudge me to become more obedient. Since I had gone my own putrid way for years before coming to know Jesus, my old habits died hard. But, alas, they did die.

Sometimes I reacted to the old scars of emotional abuse of my previous marriage, which led me to second-guess my new and loving husband's kind action of opening the door for me. I would bristle and retort, "Don't you think I could do that for myself?"

God had to continually do His work in and through me, reminding me of His loving-kindness. "My sweet, sweet daughter, your past struggles do not define you. Your old life is gone. You are a new creation in Me. I didn't just put bandages on those gaping wounds. You are completely healed and whole. I am your identity."

Moment by moment, I learned to "take captive every thought to make it obedient to Christ." I didn't want to miss out on God's best for me. As I kept my eyes on Jesus and not on my past hurts, my heart began to soften. I began to respond more and more to His Word and not to my past life experiences. The truths of the Bible, instead of the enemy's beguilement, began to take root.

"Maybe Brian wants to demean me?" I would say or think. "*No!* That's not who I am; that's not who my husband is either."

I found myself standing on God's truth, immersed in God's grace, and overwhelmed by God's mercy. My worth was found in Christ alone, which was now supported by my husband. So I let go of the baggage. I was victorious. I no longer walked in my woundedness. I was walking in greater obedience to the Lord, Adonai, my Master.

> I found myself standing on God's truth, immersed in God's grace, and overwhelmed by God's mercy.

Another of my Mom's favorite Christian authors, Elisabeth Elliot, reminded me that "delayed obedience is disobedience."

Ouch. God was really honing me in on my walk. Just when I thought I was doing well with my quiet time—my nonnegotiable face-to-face time with Jesus—He pruned deeper.

By now I once again was gainfully employed at an ad agency as vice president of account services. I loved my job; I excelled at it. The creative process, the hanging-out-of-helicopter photo shoots, the late-night printing-press-proof okays, the travel and lunches, the fun people I worked with, the media meetings, the marketing strategies, the ad campaign presentations—all of it was so gratifying. Plus, the pay wasn't bad either.

But God (my two favorite words) had different plans.

I noticed I was becoming increasingly unsettled. I couldn't put my finger on the problem, but I knew God was up to something. (He has a way of getting my attention.) Whenever a client canceled a lunch meeting, I found myself in a Wendy's parking lot under a shade tree in my Chevy Blazer, searching the BIBLE (or Basic Instructions Before Leaving Earth). As He spoke into my heart through His Word, Philippians 3:10–11 specifically came alive and is still my life verse. "I want to know Christ and the power of His resurrection and the fellowship of sharing in His suffering, becoming like Him in His death, and so somehow, attaining to the resurrection from the dead."

That word *know* in the Greek means "intimacy"; where He starts and I stop, you can't tell the difference.

Whoa.

He had a lot of work to do in and through me, but it couldn't be done without my reckless abandoning to Him. Period. Not sort of surrendering. Not when it was convenient. Mom and Elisabeth were right: "delayed obedience *is* disobedience.

I took the next step. God was urging me to leave the agency I had been instrumental in making successful. My identity had become wrapped up in twenty years of accomplishments, and I realized I was taking the credit for employees who had decided to follow Jesus. How sad is that? Thankfully, I heard God sweetly whisper in my ear, "Margo, I'm the Savior. You're not. In fact, I'm the one who keeps your heart beating and your lungs breathing. Do you wake yourself up in the morning?"

I felt a bit like Job must have felt when God was putting him in his humble human place.

So I obeyed. I left, just walking step-by-step with my eyes fixed upward. It was such exhilaration to let God be God. Many asked what I was going to do, and quite frankly, I had no idea. But I did know that God was and is *always* faithful, and He will *always* reward obedience.

> So I obeyed. I left, just walking step-by-step with my eyes fixed upward.

So I continued to do the next right thing.

Psalm 84:11–12 (NLT) had become my go-to verse. "For the Lord God is our sun and shield. He gives us grace and glory. The Lord will withhold no good thing from those who do what is right."

All those Chevy Blazer lunches had taught me to trust Him, no matter what. I was beginning to "know" Him more and more. Obedience was becoming easier and more joy filled.

I learned to live before an audience of one.

No one and nothing else mattered.

I was only responsible to act rightly before God.

I was not responsible for anyone else's reactions.

No wonder walking in obedience brings such relief.

That was a total change of mind from the way I had lived for most of my adult life.

I had been full of pleasing others.

I had wanted to be popular.

I had needed to liked.

A friend called that type of living "golden retriever" mentality. Yep, that had been me—but not anymore.

This was a time of real growth for me. I was growing through what I was going through. Psalm 42:7 says, "Deep calls to deep," and I was definitely going deeper with God. His Word would call to me, "Margo, whoever can be trusted with very little can also be trusted with much."

> I needed to be obedient in everything.

It's funny how that verse would weigh on me. I needed to be obedient in everything—in the little things as well as the big. Why was it so hard to choose right in the little things? I had rationalized. I had thought those little things were incidental, so God would totally understand my lack of follow-through, wouldn't He?

Um ... no.

God used the little things to finally transform my behavior. It all started with a squeegee. Yes, I'm talking about an implement edged with rubber for removing water from windows. My engineer husband had purchased a super-duper squeegee to scrape the water droplets from our master bathroom's glass shower. He did a yeoman's job as he meticulously swabbed, wiped, and swished away any possible hint of moisture. He strongly suggested I do the same, since it would help keep mildew and mold from growing.

That's a great idea, in theory, I thought. But when he traveled for business, my reasoning unraveled. *One day isn't gonna make any difference. I'm running late. I'll have to squeegee tomorrow. After all, he's in Germany. It's not like we're going to be video-chatting while I'm in the shower. He'll never know anyway.*

I noticed my rationalization didn't just last for a day. It took four days to come to my senses. As I was toweling off, I heard God whisper, "Margo, you're a Colossians 3 chick. Remember, you're working for Me and not for man. Not even for your husband."

I grabbed that squeegee, and with attention to detail, I voraciously rubbed horizontally and vertically with the care and expertise of a professional window washer. That decision felt good. Not only did it feel good, but it *was* good. I was doing the next right thing.

To this day, I am a top-notch, professional "squeegee-er." Very rarely do I listen to my old rationalization cassette tape, but if it starts to play, I make sure to push pause. Then I can flee temptation, run to obedience, and squeegee away. I'm sure that response pleases my husband as well.

Why is it, Lord, that I'm so easily satisfied with just getting by? Forgive me. The tug-of-war between obeying and rationalizing is very real. Help me to desire not only to read Your Word but also to respond. I know it's the only book that reads me as I read it. It is Your living Word. Thank You for bringing me to the end of myself. It's not always easy, but it sure is joyful. I want to please You. Help me to do the next right thing.

Devotions
for Your Next Right Steps

Learning to Obey

Overflowing Enthusiasm
Listen. Respond. Act.
God's Big House
God-Style Refreshment
God-Issued Weapons

Overflowing Enthusiasm

> Write these commandments that I've given you today on your hearts. Get them inside of you and then get them inside your children. Talk about them wherever you are, sitting at home or walking in the street; talk about them from the time you get up in the morning to when you fall into bed at night. Tie them on your hands and foreheads as a reminder; inscribe them on the doorposts of your homes and on your city gates.
>
> —Deuteronomy 6:6–9 (MSG)

When life bumps into you (and it will), what spills out of you?

Blame?

Excuses?

Critical words?

Or are you spilling out

Acceptance?

Gratefulness?

Humility?

God's Word?

It's what's already inside you that spills out.

If a pitcher is full of milk, milk will spill out of it, since milk is already inside the pitcher. If you knock over a glass of water, what splashes all over the counter? Certainly not orange juice. And the same principle is true for our lives. What's inside you will spill out of you, whether you want it to or not.

That's why Moses encouraged us to "write the commandments on your heart. Get them inside of you and *inside* of your children" (emphasis mine).

And how do you do that? Well, he went on to tell us. "Talk about them wherever you are."

That means not just at church or during bedtime prayers at night. It means wherever you are, so if you're waiting at the school bus, talk about them. If you're making cookies, talk about them. If you're helping with homework, talk about them.

Therefore, you need to be familiar with His commandments yourself. If you're going to talk about "something" with another, you need to know about that "something."

> God's commandments and promises need to be hidden in your heart.

God's Word, His very commandments and promises, need to be hidden in your heart. That is, they need to be in your mind, will, and emotions. Then you will overflow with talking about Him "from the time you get up in the morning to when you fall into bed at night."

Sharing truths from God's Word won't be on your to-do checklist anymore. You just can't help yourself. Your passion for God will run deep. Your children (and others around you) will catch that passion as you are overflowing from the inside out.

Overflow with acceptance, gratefulness, humility, and God's Word.

Listen. Respond. Act.

> Don't fool yourself into thinking that you are a listener when you are anything but, letting the Word go in one ear and out the other. Act on what you hear! Those who hear and don't act are like those who glance in the mirror, walk away, and two minutes later have no idea who they are, what they look like.
>
> —James 1:22–24 (MSG)

Would you consider yourself a good listener—an active listener? When someone addresses you, do you look him or her in the eye? Nod? Understand what the person is saying and then respond appropriately?

> You hear from the Father that a bad habit needs to go; do something about it.

What about when "the Someone" is talking to you? When God's living and active Word speaks into the very depth of your being? Whether you're reading it, a pastor is preaching it, a teacher is teaching it, or you're in conversation with Him, are those listening skills tuned up? Is His Word going in one ear and out the other?

In the NIV translation, James 1 says, "Do not merely listen to the Word and so deceive yourselves. Do what it says."

When His very Word is convicting you, don't turn away. That's the equivalent of looking in a mirror and two minutes later forgetting what you look like. What good did it do to look in the mirror if you're not going to respond to what the mirror pointed out? Spinach in your teeth. Mascara weeping. Toilet paper stuck to your heel. Static cling. You wouldn't ignore what you saw reflected. You'd correct it and be grateful for the mirror.

It's the same principle with active listening. You hear from the Father that a bad habit needs to go; your words need to be cleaned up; an apology must be said. Do something about it.

After all, He has left His living and active Word so we can thrive in the abundant life He desires for us, a purpose-filled life.

Don't fool yourself into thinking you're a listener when you're not.

Act on what you hear.

God's Big House

> One day spent in your house, this beautiful place of worship, beats thousands spent on Greek island beaches. I'd rather scrub floors in the house of my God than be honored as a guest in the palace of sin. All sunshine and sovereign is God, generous in gifts and glory. He doesn't scrimp with his traveling companions. It's smooth sailing all the way with God-of-the-Angel-Armies.
>
> —Psalm 84:10–12 (MSG)

Are you in a close, personal, ever-growing love relationship with God?

I mean, are you in the kind of relationship that can say, as David said, that he would rather spend one day—just one—in God's house than spend it on thousands of gorgeous white-sand beaches?

Would you trade Greek island beaches, thousands of them, for one day in God's beautiful place of worship?

The decision isn't about the places. It comes down to who is in that place. Oh, absolutely, God's house is gloriously beautiful, but the big deal is that God is there. I mean, you would be with God Himself.

Oh, that would be glory for me—looking at His face, falling before Him in worship.

If only for a day. (Even though I know I will eventually spend every day forever with Him.)

"How would you feel about trading being an honored guest in a palace of iniquity for scrubbing floors in God's house?"

Hmm ... a guest in a palace or doing manual labor in a house? That would be a no-brainer except for the fact that God Almighty lives in that house.

Scrubbing floors in God's house comes with huge dividends. God is generous in gifts and glory.

And He doesn't scrimp.

And He loves to reward you.

And you'd be in the presence of God.

And that's enough! What if you find yourself being more attracted to thousands of white-sand beaches and being a guest of honor in a palace of sin than desiring to be in the house of God?

If that is your quandary, He is calling you to go deeper with Him.

And to know Him more.

And to fall in love with Him.

He wants to be your everything because He gave His everything (Jesus) for you to walk over His heavenly threshold.

**He did it all for you
so you could give your all to Him.**

God-Style Refreshment

> In your great love revive me so I can alertly obey your every word. What you say goes, God, and stays, as permanent as the heavens. Your truth never goes out of fashion; it's as up-to-date as the earth when the sun comes up. Your Word and truth are dependable as ever; that's what you ordered—you set the earth going.
>
> —Psalm 119:88–91 (MSG)

How are you revived, rejuvenated, and refreshed? Does a well-timed nap help? A day at the spa? A walk with your pup? Calling your close friend? How about kneeling in prayer?

The psalmist David knew God's great love—His unconditional love—would revive him. And where did he run to personally experience that love? God's great love story—a.k.a. God's Word, the Bible.

He had the settled joy and hope that what God says goes. No debate. No doubt. No deterring.

Just trusting in God's unfailing permanent-as-the-heavens Word.

That's why he could be revived. David didn't wish what God had said was true. He knew. He declared that his personal Yahweh, God and His spoken Word, is truth and as dependable as ever.

David knew where to run to be brought back to life. He knew who would revive him. Before David needed to be refreshed, he knew the Refresher. That's important. If you don't know who to run to before you need Him, you will end up stewing in your circumstances or running aimlessly after all the wrong things and wrong people.

And here's the clincher. What was David's purpose in being revived? "So I can alertly obey your every word!"

He ran to God's Word to be revived so he could know His every word. Why? To obey. To do the next right thing.

> He ran to God's Word to be revived so he could know His every word.

What?
Yep, there's the answer to being revived:
Know God.
Know His Word.
Be revived.
Obey His Word to
Know God,
Know His Word,
Be revived.
Obey His Word to
Know God,
Know His Word,
Be revived.
(Repeat until you see Jesus face-to-face.) That is real refreshment God style, and the deeper you go with Him, the deeper will be your personal revival.

**His Word will never fail you,
only rejuvenate.**

God-Issued Weapons

Be prepared. You're up against far more than you can handle on your own. Take all the help you can get, every weapon God has issued, so that when it's all over but the shouting you'll still be on your feet. Truth, righteousness, peace, faith, and salvation are more than words. Learn how to apply them. You'll need them throughout your life. God's Word is an indispensable weapon. In the same way, prayer is essential in this ongoing warfare. Pray hard and long. Pray for your brothers and sisters. Keep your eyes open. Keep each other's spirits up so that no one falls behind or drops out.

—Ephesians 6:13–18 (MSG)

If I need weapons, that must mean I'm in a battle. Weapons aren't issued for idyllic times. And God Himself has issued me specific weapons. My job is to take and use them so I'm always prepared for an attack—a bold, in-my-face attack or a sneaky, behind-my-back attack. Regardless of which one, I will still be standing when it's all said and done.

God's weapons don't seem like weapons to me. They seem more like clothing. They are things I put on that cover me. That's it.

His weapons do all the work, just like I put on Under Armour to keep the cold away. It's the inherent nature of Under Armour to be my weapon against the cold. It's the same with God's weapons. They are His nature, which I "put on"; and He protects me from the battles that rage against me.

However, I need to take His weapons, recognizing that I need all the help I can get. Just like the battle of staying warm in a polar vortex of frigid, negative double-digit temperatures. I can know all about Under Armour and how it works to stay the cold, but if I don't take that "weapon" and put it on, I certainly won't be prepared. My body is up against far more than it can handle on its own.

God's weapons are for a lifetime of use. They never wear out. They will always blaze the way before me and protect me. (Remember—"Take all the help you can get, every weapon God has issued, so that when it's all over but the shouting you'll still be on your feet.")

> God's weapons are for a lifetime of use.

Truth always wins out.

Righteousness (being right with God) is a gift for the taking.

Peace, the peace of God that passes all understanding, will guard your hearts and minds in Christ Jesus.

Faith takes God at His word and acts on it.

Salvation assures us that we walk with God here and live forever with God there.

God's Word, the Bible, will be on the attack, allowing you to be strong in what you say and do.

Prayer, two-way communication with your most-high General, is essential for navigating through the battles. If that communication is damaged, you will wander aimlessly into enemy territory, making you a prime target.

Why wouldn't you want to keep in constant communication with the one who can give you victory? Who sees the big picture instead of the little snapshot you see? Keep your eyes open. See what He sees. Take your God-issued weapons. Be prepared. Read His victory log, the Bible.

And pray, because, as Jim Elliot said,

"That saint who advances on his knees never retreats!"

Chapter 5

God Always Has "Plan A"

DINKS: Dual Income, No Kids.

That was us. We appreciated eight years of wedded bliss. Plus, the sweat equity we had put into our first home had paid off, allowing us to now live in a much-welcome lake home. I joyfully taught a hundred kids about Jesus every Sunday, while Brian led worship, teaching them all the stanzas to "Awesome God" by Rich Mullins, because it was his favorite. Both of us were involved in men's and women's ministries and hosted a small group in our home.

We were growing vertically in Jesus and horizontally with each other.

It was around this time that a friend gave me a hysterical card that looked like an old comic book. The woman was smacking her forehead with a bubble that said, "Oh! I forgot to have kids!"

It was innocently meant to be funny, but it really rattled me.

Oh wow, I thought.

Brian and I started to get real with God and each other about becoming parents. We realized it was now or perhaps never.

Follow Jesus.

Do the next right thing.

We were excited.

However, we experienced four years of excruciatingly painful infertility. We certainly hadn't expected that to be the case since we were both in excellent health. But we hung onto the fact that God still had His best plan for us. So a complete infertility workup was done on me. Thankfully, Brian was fine. It was me. I didn't have enough progesterone to carry the baby past the delicate first trimester.

We had one miscarriage that was very early term, maybe six weeks along. On our way home from a full day of shopping for our first ski boat, we stopped for lunch, and it was there that I miscarried on the toilet in the restaurant's public restroom.

Physical pain.

Emotional pain.

Such pain.

Through tears, we held each other and prayed to the one who was holding us.

Nobody knew our crushing heartache but the two of us, so we grieved alone in the middle of the hopping lunch rush, holding onto the hope that we'd meet our precious child in heaven someday. Plus, we were reminded that early-term miscarriages are common. However, since I was considered high risk, we had more detailed workups done. In the meantime, we got pregnant again. This time the regimen included all the progesterone boosters: butt cheek shots daily (that was fun) plus orally and through suppositories.

The treatments helped me get past the fragile first trimester. Exhilarated, I was able to feel life inside me for the first time.

What joy—only to have her life cut short at twenty weeks. We went in for a routine checkup. There was trouble. We had waited such a long time to be called "Mom" and "Dad," and now our dream was put on hold. Friends, family and coworkers were over-the-moon excited for us, but it was over.

Even Brian's workplace had thrown a surprise baby shower for us, including all the must-haves and adorable pink everything.

I had just begun to feel life inside me. I had been praising the one who allowed me to have that miraculous experience. I was so humbled by the fact that I could be carrying life in me, and then there was no life. The medical world labeled me a "habitual aborter."

> I had just begun to feel life inside me.

At that point, I remember very clearly that I had a choice. I was either going to draw nearer to the one I knew had created that gift of life I was housing. Or I was going to be angry, falsely blaming God for being the one who didn't allow our baby girl to be our firstborn daughter.

I immediately chose to trust God.

Immediately.

It was a real coming-to-Jesus moment when I believed I loved Him not only in the good times but also in the not-so-good times. He is faithful no matter what. God's Word sweetly reminded me that "His mercies are new every morning," so I chose to follow hard after Him.

After all, He was my first love, and these circumstances somehow and someway would be used for my good and His glory. My job was to trust the living God, who knows the end from the beginning. And so I did, knowing He had good in store for me—not only for me but for my husband and our eventual God-given family. He wasn't about to abandon me now. And I wasn't about to abandon Him.

Our relationship was an eternal commitment, so I asked Him through tears, "Jesus, what do You want me to learn through this?"

I went through twenty-five hours of agonizing labor on labor-inducing medications, knowing this precious baby inside me had already moved to heaven. It was only her earthly shell I was birthing, which required a morphine drip due to intense pain. I asked to be taken off it since I felt like I was under water and wanted to be totally aware when she arrived.

She was stillborn.

So tiny.

So pink.

Actually, red. Less than two pounds. Wrapped in a newborn blanket. We held her and wept—and named her Angela. It was a perfect name since it means "messenger of God." God had sent her to a hurting couple for such a time as this. And so we thanked Him for her, for our changed lives, and for going deeper in our relationship with Him and each other.

The hospital treated her sacred little body just as though her soul were still in it. They gave her height and weight, and put on a tiny knit hat and blanket. A picture of a dove was put on our door to let others know a soul had left that room. Really, she had left some time ago.

Angela seemed perfect, except she was so small. Brian held her as we whispered and whimpered conversations to the one who was still holding us, just as we still held her.

We had a tender graveside service for Angela, actually more for us, and buried her on top of my dad's grave. My mom, sister, brother-in-law, and funeral director all huddled around Brian and me on a chilly February day. Her daddy held her minuscule casket as Sandi Patty's voice flowed out of the boom box, singing "Another Time, Another Place."

That song's lyrics were absolutely perfect—"swept away to another time and another place." Angela had immediately been born in heaven.

No pain.

No sorrow.

Forever with Jesus.

She would be forever with the very one that was depicted on her bronze plaque that memorialized her. It was a sculpted picture of children on Jesus's lap. The plaque was inscribed,

Angela Fieseler
Born to Another Time, Another Place
February 23, 1993

We learned that I would easily be able to get pregnant but would be unable to carry a baby to full term. That label "habitual aborter" was such an ugly phrase to me, and my heart grieved even from the sound of those words.

We worked hard to remember that hope doesn't rest in a child—it rests in Jesus.

Somehow, someway, through my tears, I knew the words "God always has plan A" were true. God always has His best plan, even when I can't see it through my snapshot-of-my-world eyes. He sees the end from the beginning and the beginning from the end. Nothing takes God by surprise.

Once again, Mom's words gave me comfort. "God allows everything for our good and His glory."

Throughout the grieving process, reality hit me like crashing waves of the sea. Why were we burying our baby instead of watching her blond hair bounce to and fro as she skipped down the hill with our collie? My gut wrenched, but I clung to the truth in His Word. God is good all the time. All the time He is good. I knew He was just as good now as He had been before Angela died. He couldn't be anything else but good. He's a good, good Father. "How kind the Lord is! How good He is! So merciful, this God of ours! Let my soul be at rest again, for the Lord has been good to me. And so I walk in the Lord's presence as I live here on earth! The Lord cares deeply when His loved ones die" (Psalm 116:5, 7, 9, 15 NLT).

Like never before, this psalm was full of such sweet morsels of truth for me.

I would cry aloud.

I would whisper.

I would wrestle.

He would calm me time and time again. "Margo, I always have My best plans for you. Keep your eyes on Me. I will never fail you."

Then His Word would flood my soul. "Taste and see that the Lord is good. Oh, the joys of those who take refuge in Him!" (Psalm 34:8 NLT).

Ahh, the psalmist brought more sweet refreshment. The Lord was my sanctuary.

My haven.

My fortress.

My hiding place.

The longer I lingered with Him, the more my taste buds began to savor and see that the Lord is good. Always. He is not good only if my prayer is answered according to my wants.

He continued to remind me, "And we know that in all things God works for the good of those who love him, who have been called according to his purpose" (Romans 8:28 NIV). I knew that verse was talking directly to me.

In God's loving-kindness, He brought me to the end of my plans to the absolute knowing that His plan A was continually, everlastingly without exception the best plan. That's when I gave God the rightful place in my life.

Falling face-first on our bed, with tears streaming down my already red-blotched face, I waved the white flag of surrender. "Jesus, I love You. If we never have kids, I know that I know You still have your best plan for me. Even though I don't see, I choose to believe Your Word is true" (just like my mom would have lovingly advised me years before).

> It became apparently evident that following His plan A would include conforming me to the likeness of His Son.

It became apparently evident that following His plan A would include conforming me to the likeness of His Son. After all, that is part of His whole redemptive plan—to save me and clean up every room in my home, including the messy ones, such as the basement, attic, and garage.

Not more than two months after Angela's stillbirth, I would experience another unexpected physical trauma. In the middle of enjoying chicken Caesar salad at Applebee's with my husband and his coworkers, prior to an Easter production at church, I looked down and exclaimed, "I'm hemorrhaging!" My purple pants had turned to red—just that quickly.

Servers panicked.

An ambulance was called.

Oxygen went into place.

An IV was started.

I was whisked onto a gurney and rolled through the restaurant while giving the thumbs-up sign to hopefully still the patrons' hearts (and mine).

I knew that I knew God was in control, even though I didn't know what was happening or why. But it didn't matter anymore. I was in the Lord of all creation's hands. And I would be okay no matter what.

In the emergency room I began singing familiar praise songs, such as "Our God Is an Awesome God" and "I Love You, Lord." The attending nurses and doctor sang along since they were from our church. What a hug from heaven. After two units of blood and a three-day stay, I was released.

The findings regarding why I hemorrhaged were "major complications" resulting from Angela's still birth several weeks earlier. The complications meant that the hemorrhaging could have occurred at any moment or day. Brian and I were to have flown out early the next morning for some much-needed rest and relaxation at our favorite place on earth: Maui. God certainly had His best plan for me. The emergency room doctor remarked that if I had been on that planned United flight to Maui—if I had made it that one more day before this medical issue occurred, rather than having my Applebee's emergency—it would have been my last day on earth.

God always has plan A.

Our plans were to fly to Maui.

God's plan A, keeping me safe on the ground, was so much better.

Meanwhile, His loving-kindness kept drawing me to Himself—not in ways I would have imagined but in a way the Father knows best. His Word spoke to my soul. "I will instruct you and teach you in the way you should go; I will counsel you with my loving eye on you" (Psalm 32:8 NIV). Thankfully, I was learning to listen to His still small voice.

He would instruct me.

He would teach me the way to go.

He was making my crooked path straight.

So when I became pregnant again, for the third time, I trusted Him for the outcome. However, this precious baby, like Angela, was also born to "another time and another place." I miscarried during my first trimester.

Meanwhile, across a couple of states, my mother-in-law, Gladys, had a back surgery that went terribly wrong. She died twice on the table. In fact, the doctors scrambled to save her life and in the process damaged numerous organs. She was in the intensive care unit for six months—not six days or six weeks but six months. They had given her a 10 percent chance of living.

At that time, my mom's heartfelt, handwritten letter showed up at Gladys's bedside. By now my husband was at his mom's side, praying for a miracle and reading the letter aloud. The nurse had read it to her once, but she requested to hear it again. Who wouldn't? My mom's Holy Spirit-written words were a balm to Gladys's soul.

Mom wrote that she was praying, believing that God would do "exceedingly, abundantly more than we can ask or think." She wrote that Father God, the Good Shepherd, would comfort her; that Jesus would be her Great Physician and Healer. And then Mom intimately shared her own journey of accepting Jesus as her personal Savior, making sure to exclaim, "Not once have I ever regretted that decision."

Unconditional love poured in and through mom's supernatural words that had begun to pierce Gladys's heart. Brian bent over closer to his mom and whispered, "Wouldn't you like to know Jesus like Mary does? If you died tonight, wouldn't you want to be in heaven with Jesus forever? Wouldn't you like to accept Jesus in your life? He is waiting for you."

Even though Gladys was intubated, she motioned for the handheld chalkboard and painstakingly wrote, "I already have."

Tears of joy poured down Brian's face. God's word, through the compassionate heart of my mom, had melted Gladys's heart. The Hound of Heaven, Jesus, was after that one lost sheep. "Rejoice with me; I have found my lost sheep. I tell you that in the same way there will be more rejoicing in heaven over one sinner who repents than over ninety-nine righteous persons who do not need to repent" (Luke 15:6–7 NIV). I'm sure I could hear the angels celebrating over Gladys, the "one sinner who repents."

I will always remember how Gladys held tightly to my mom's letter. She later explained that she knew she was dying and was going to show Jesus the letter when she arrived at heaven's door, because she believed every word of it. It was her get-out-of-jail-free pass. But this would last forever.

Plus, as my father-in-law was driving Brian back to the airport, he came to know Jesus, too.

Brian asked his dad, "Don't you want to know Jesus like mom does?"

His simple reply: "Yes."

Faith as a little child.

That's how it happens in Acts 16:31, "Believe in the Lord Jesus, and you will be saved" (Acts 16:31 NIV).

Oh, and my mother-in-law? She didn't move to heaven. Instead she and her husband moved from Iowa to Wisconsin, just a couple of miles away from our home. Not only is her soul well, but her body is too.

I'm so grateful, my good, good Father, that You always have plan A. And it's Your best plan specifically designed for me. I know You are teaching me to trust You in the midst of the good, the bad, and the ugly. Continue to soften my heart so I can see more clearly through eyes of faith, knowing Your plans aren't to harm me but to give me hope and a future. I refuse to settle for my second best. Thank You for taking me safely through the storms to the other side.

Devotions
for Your Next Right Steps

God Is Good...All the Time

Overwhelms Me with His Goodness
The Source of Every Good Thing
Permeated with Good
The Gift of Trying Times
No Febreze Needed

Overwhelms Me with His Goodness

So we're not giving up. How could we! Even though on the outside it often looks like things are falling apart on us, on the inside, where God is making new life, not a day goes by without his unfolding grace. These hard times are small potatoes compared to the coming good times, the lavish celebration prepared for us. There's far more here than meets the eye. The things we see now are here today, gone tomorrow. But the things we can't see now will last forever.

—2 Corinthians 4:16–18 (MSG)

"Don't give up! You can do it! Keep your eyes on the prize. You're almost there. It will be so worth it. Don't quit now! Keep on!"

It's almost as if I can hear God cheering me on in this earthly grind. And He is, you know. He pours out His grace (undeserved favor) upon grace upon grace upon grace over me, making new life in me.

Even though our earthly tents are wasting away, inwardly we're being renewed day by day, so there is absolutely no reason to give up. His grace sustains us and overwhelms us with His goodness.

After all, our insides are our real selves. Our outsides are just the vehicles to house and transport our insides. So why is it that we spend so much time and money on the part that is falling apart on us?

The things we see now are here today and gone tomorrow. Temporary. My financial planner wouldn't advise me to invest in that stock. No long-lasting dividends. Just dust in the wind.

"But the things we can't see now will last forever."

That truth should bring a smile to your face. As I focus on God, walking by faith and not by sight, my spirit never gives up. My spirit recognizes that present troubles are small and don't last very long.

> A lavish celebration is being prepared for me.

I am able by God's ever-flowing grace to walk through hard times and realize they are small potatoes compared to the coming good times. A lavish celebration is being prepared for me.

There is no reason under the Son to give up and every reason to keep on. Remember, you are being renewed inside day by day, no matter how your outside is falling apart on you.

His grace is sufficient.
Walk by the Spirit.

The Source of Every Good Thing

> Speaking to the people, he went on, 'Take care! Protect yourself against the least bit of greed. Life is not defined by what you have, even when you have a lot." Then he told them this story: 'The farm of a certain rich man produced a terrific crop. He talked to himself: 'What can I do? My barn isn't big enough for this harvest.' Then he said, 'Here's what I'll do: I'll tear down my barns and build bigger ones. Then I'll gather in all my grain and goods, and I'll say to myself, Self, you've done well! You've got it made and can now retire. Take it easy and have the time of your life!' Just then God showed up and said, 'Fool! Tonight you die. And your barnful of goods—who gets it?' That's what happens when you fill your barn with Self and not with God."
>
> —Luke 12:15–21 (MSG)

Do you find yourself always wanting more? Are you consumed with wanting more wealth or possessions? If so, God calls you a fool—and here's why: "Life is not defined by what you have, even if you have a lot."

Many are defined by their stuff. Famed economist Malcolm Forbes is attributed with the often-repeated saying that the person with the most toys at the end of his or her life wins. Really? That's your focus? That's your purpose? No wonder God calls this type of person a fool; he or she is too busy filling his or her life with self and not God. Ugh.

The rich man was so consumed with his big harvest, patting himself on the back, building a new barn to hold all his "stuff," and gathering in all his grain and goods. While he was congratulating himself about his early retirement, God appeared on the scene, reminding him that he had spent his entire life with the wrong focus.

"All on me, me, me! Look at me! I've got it made. All my riches. All my abundance. All my ability. And now I'm gonna really live! Take it easy and have the time of my life."

Um, not so much. He's forgetting one thing, one very important thing. *God is in control.* God is the one who gives you the ability to make wealth. "You may say to yourself, 'My power and the strength of my hands have produced this wealth for me.' But remember the Lord your God, for it is he who gives you the ability to produce wealth" (Deuteronomy 8:17–18 NIV).

No wonder God called the rich man a fool. He wasted his life on himself. And that very night his life was demanded of him. What did he have to show for all his efforts? Nothing. He had nothing that would last forever.

This verse begs the question: What are you filling your barn with? Self or God? Only you can answer that. And one day we will have to answer before God. It is so much better to answer that question now.

**Life is not defined by what you have.
Fill yourself with God.**

Permeated with Good

> Yes! God is good! His love never quits!
>
> —2 Chronicles 7:3 (MSG)

Do you walk every day absolutely assured that "God is good. His love never quits"? Can you shout a loud, "Yes," to others around you, without wavering?

If you struggle with this truth, I suggest you get to know Him more.

His character.

His changelessness.

He is God. He is innately good. He is immutably good.

That means God can't be anything but good. He is only good ... all the time. Good isn't something He does; it is His very being. God is good. He isn't swayed by this or that, or by your actions. He is God. He is good. Period.

> God can't be anything but good.

God doesn't have to try to "be good," like we do. He doesn't need to be taught to "do the next right thing." His very nature is permeated with good. He cannot not be good.

So for whatever circumstance He allows in your life, it originated in God's goodness. I can hear you saying, "But what about this trial with my child I'm going through?" or "My sister has just been diagnosed with cancer. How can that be good?"

God isn't saying that all circumstances are going to feel good. Sadly, we live in a sin-infested, less-than-perfect— as the Bible calls it, "fallen"—world. *But God* (there are those two favorite words again) will use those very situations for "the good." He will make good out of bad. "And we know that in all things God works for the good of those who love Him, who have been called according to His purpose" (Romans 8:28 NIV).

Look at Joseph's life—from the favored son to a slave and back to the man in charge. In Genesis 50:20, Joseph revealed himself to his wayward brothers (who had sold him and told Dad he was dead), saying, "You intended this for bad, *but God* intended it for good ... for the saving of many" (emphasis mine).

As you read Joseph's life story, you'll see that his circumstances looked anything but good. *But God* (have I mentioned those are my two favorite words?) used them for his good. Joseph knew God. He knew God was good. He trusted that this always-good God, in whatever life experience He brought him through, would be for his good and God's glory.

God is good all the time. All the time God is good. Oh, and here's the icing on the cake: "His love never quits." In this ever-changing world, there are two unchanging facts you can shout, "Yes" to:

God is good all the time.
His love never quits.

The Gift of Trying Times

> Consider it a sheer gift, friends, when tests and challenges come at you from all sides. You know that under pressure, your faith-life is forced into the open and shows its true colors. So don't try to get out of anything prematurely. Let it do its work so you become mature and well-developed, not deficient in any way.
>
> —James 1:2–4 (MSG)

Okay, so do you think it's a gift from the hand of God when tests and challenges come at you from all sides? I'm sure sometimes we all respond, "Not so much."

James said we're to consider a trial a sheer gift from God.

Huh?

I know. I used to balk at trials, tests, and challenges. Thoughts would rush through my mind. *Why is this happening to me?* And I would do whatever I could to shorten the hardship I was experiencing. But thankfully, as my faith grows up, I do, too.

After all, how am I gonna grow up in my faith if it isn't tested? If everything is always hunky dory, I'll be able to muster through, except the problem with that approach is that I think I have conquered my test all on my own.

Meanwhile, when I'm under pressure, my faith life is forced into the open, showing its true colors. Plus, others are watching this faith walking and not sight walking like a hawk. They want to see whether what I say is what I do.

They want to see whether I'm a mess.

If I'm anxious.

If I'm fearful.

If my faith is going to conquer my feelings, because faith is not a feeling. "And it is impossible to please God without faith. Anyone who wants to come to him must believe that God exists and that he rewards those who sincerely seek him" (Hebrews 11:6 NLT).

> Let your faith be tested and let it do its work.

So let your faith be tested and let it do its work so you may become mature and well developed, not deficient in any way.

When I'm able to accept that everything God allows in my life is for my good and His glory—the good and the bad, the happy and the sad—then my focus is right. I am trusting the unseen. I've zeroed in on my big God; therefore, my correct response is,

What are You teaching me through this test?
What do You want me to learn?

No Febreze Needed

And so I insist—and God backs me up on this—that there be no going along with the crowd, the empty-headed, mindless crowd. They've refused for so long to deal with God that they've lost touch not only with God but with reality itself. They can't think straight anymore. ...But that's no life for you. You learned Christ!... Since, then, we do not have the excuse of ignorance, everything—and I do mean everything—connected with that old way of life has to go. It's rotten through and through. Get rid of it! And then take on an entirely new way of life—a God-fashioned life, a life renewed from the inside and working itself into your conduct as God accurately reproduces his character in you.

—Ephesians 4:17–24 (MSG)

"Character is what a man is in the dark," D. L. Moody said. When no one is looking and you are all alone, who are you? Are you still living an old, rotten way of life or an entirely new way of life?

One way is like the empty-headed, mindless crowd that has refused for so long to deal with God that they can't think straight anymore. The other is an entirely new way of life, a God-fashioned life renewed from the inside and working itself into your conduct as God accurately reproduces His character in you.

The apostle Paul said right from the start (talking to Jesus followers), and God backs him up, that you aren't to have anything to do with that old, rotten life. Ignorance is no excuse.

Why would you want to return to old ways, bad habits, and mindless actions? That's what your character used to be before you invited Christ into your life. He's not there to take a back seat. No. He's there to drive. He's there to take over, and you can enjoy the ride as "God reproduces His character in you!"

> Why would you want to return to old ways, bad habits, and mindless actions?

And that's the best part. He doesn't take your old character and place bandages all over it, trying to mend or cover up the old wounds and scars.

No, He makes you brand new because that old life was rotten through and through; bandages would only temporarily cover up your sores. But the stench emitting from the inside cannot be covered. That needs an inside cure.

A whole transformation.

Enter Jesus.

He makes all things new.

Febreze doesn't just cover up the stench of your old character. No, He has gone deep inside, from where the source of the stench emanates. And He has given you a clean heart, one that belongs to Him.

His character is working itself into your conduct.

Chapter 6

Trusting the Unseen

You may never know that Jesus is all you need, until Jesus is all you have.

—Corrie ten Boom

Corrie ten Boom not only said this quote but also lived it. Known for hiding many Jews in her family home, Corrie helped them escape the Nazi Holocaust during World War II. She and her sister, Betsie, were imprisoned for their heroic actions and sent to Ravensbrück concentration camp, a women's labor camp in Germany. Before Betsie died there, she told Corrie, "There is no pit so deep that (God) is not deeper still."

Fifteen days later Corrie was released due to a clerical error. Just one week after that, all the women in her age-group were sent to the gas chambers.

Corrie told the story of her family and their World War II work in her best-selling book, *The Hiding Place* (1971). It was one of my mom's favorite books and is now mine as well.

How did Corrie walk through unthinkable conditions and deplorable abuse? She trusted the unseen. The "seen" was horrific, but she could see through her eyes of faith beyond her gruesome, frightful, and dire circumstances.

That's just what I decided to do. Trust the unseen. No, I've never experienced the atrocities Corrie did, but I decided that no matter what would come along, I would trust that God either allowed it or caused it for my good and His glory.

That's pretty much what life is about this side of heaven. You're going into a problem, you're in a problem, or you're coming out of a problem. It's how you walk through your problems that makes all the difference in the world.

I had learned through daily study in God's Word to resolve (to already have decided) to trust the one who is totally trustworthy before trouble comes along.

Oh, and trouble will come along. Jesus said, "In the world you will have trouble. But take heart! I have overcome the world" (John 16:33 NIV).

After the loss of my three babies, my heart's desire was still to have a family, and I wasn't getting any younger. The big difference was that I had now given the matter over to the one who had His best plan for me.

And so I prayed.

And waited.

But this time I was waiting in God's waiting room.

God's waiting room was safe and peaceful as I snuggled up on His lap. I continued to give God His rightful place in my life. I knew He was able to bring me a baby, but I needed to trust Him in the "how" and "now."

When I read an excerpt from *Prayer That Works* by Jill Briscoe, my friend and mentor, she reminded me, "When you pray, there are two things you cannot tell God. You can't tell Him *how*, and you can't tell Him *now*."

And so I continued to trust and wait.

I knew having a biological baby wasn't advisable after all the trauma my body had experienced, so I believed God was up to something else. I found myself singing a childhood hymn (by Louisa M. R. Stead), not surprisingly since I had heard my mom sing it almost daily as we cleaned the house.

> I continued to obediently hang out in God's waiting room.

> 'Tis so sweet to trust in Jesus,
> Just to take Him at His Word.
> Just to rest upon His promise,
> Just to know, "Thus saith the Lord."
> Jesus, Jesus, how I trust Him!
> How I've proved Him o'er and o'er
> Jesus, Jesus, precious Jesus!
> Oh, for grace to trust Him more.

It was sweet to trust the unseen, to trust Jesus. He was changing me moment by moment to reflect more of Him and less of me.

More compassion.

More love.

More others oriented.

He was preparing me for what lay ahead.

Then it happened. Just when I least expected it, Jesus showed up big time at our Bible study waterski get-together at our home. My sister, Marney, shared with me that she knew of a nineteen-year-old who was pregnant and didn't want to parent the baby. I turned to her and uttered, "I would love that baby in a heartbeat."

As I continued to hostess, I prayed, "If this baby is ours, then God, You need to make it very clear. I'm not running ahead of You."

Marney excitedly followed up later that week, with the pregnant woman's e-mail address. All the while I kept petitioning God, crying out, "Lord, I'm not contacting this woman unless this is directly from You. I've chosen to put my hope in You alone, not in this child. If this is Your open door, I'm going to nudge on it, just a bit, and if it swings wide open, I know that I know You are speaking."

I didn't blast the door down. I ever so slightly touched the door—I e-mailed her. It was something very easy and sweet, acknowledging she was with child and that my sister had shared her news with me, since we were looking to adopt. I included a favorite poem of mine by Jill Briscoe about waiting. I told her I was praying for her in every way and that all "children are a heritage from the Lord" (Psalm 127:3 NIV). I just wanted to give her hope so that no matter what she chose, she would desire to give that precious child life. To my delight, she replied to my e-mail that same day.

"It's great to hear from you!" she began, carefully writing that she had been bowled over by my words. What an unexpected response. From that time on, we communicated quite often, talking about her doctor appointments and how her pregnancy was progressing, including her peculiar late-night cravings.

Such sweet details, I thought as I continued to obediently hang out in God's waiting room. I began to realize that "for such a time as this," we were more than potential matches through a child. God had a bigger plan and purpose as Brian and I continued to walk the up-and-down journey, never quite sure where the winding road would take us. Thankfully, we chose to give it over to the one who did know the outcome. We asked God to speak into her life, no matter what it meant for our future. Eventually, I introduced my husband and our "firstborn," a collie, through e-mails. Finally, we decided to meet.

We suggested a big buffet restaurant in Madison, which was thankfully to her liking. As we sat across from each other, our conversation was lively, truthful, tearful, and joy filled. She chatted about her job, her family, and her pregnancy.

We listened.

We poured into her.

We listened some more.

As we were walking her to her car, I slipped *What to Expect When Expecting* and a Bible into her hands. Our eyes met, and we both teared up.

What a good, good Father we have.

So Brian and I kept walking forward ever so faithfully through God's ever-widening door, unaware of the many other infertile couples who had come out of the woodwork when she was pregnant, announcing their desire to adopt the little one. Her heart, though, was already decided; she knew she was carrying the baby for us.

Sooner than I could have conceived, carried, and delivered a child, the call came in.

Our trusty minivan was outfitted with all the newborn necessities; our collie was ready to jump in the "car-car" and I was in the middle of baking a cake. Really? (I *never* bake cakes.) The biological mom called to exclaim, "Hurry. Hurry. I'm in the hospital!" She wanted us to be at the birth. I remember saying, "But Brian, we have twenty minutes before the cake is done."

It's like I couldn't believe it was really happening, but my calm, engineer husband put his arm around me and said, "Just turn off the oven, hon."

It was -11 degrees that morning on February 11 when we arrived in the hospital's parking structure. We checked in at the front desk and hurried up the steps and down the maternity unit hall to her LDRP (Labor Delivery Recovery Postpartum) room.

Turn off the stove.

Drop off the dog.

Get to the hospital.

We were quick but not quick enough. We had missed the birth by an hour. When I walked into her room, my eyes quickly glanced around at her family and friends surrounding her bedside. She smiled and sweetly welcomed us, introducing us to everyone as the baby's parents.

I remember placing this tiny, perfect baby girl in my husband's arms as he was longingly waiting in the rocking chair. He couldn't take his eyes off our daughter, our Becca. Joy erupted all over his face. It must have been a special moment in time, just between the two of them, since he never noticed everyone else hugging, talking, laughing, and crying all at once— her big family and our new little one. Time passed quickly for everybody else, but Brian sat in a bubble with his little bundle of joy. A gift from God.

My heart was full.

Daddy and his daughter.

Now and forever

A bond made in heaven.

Then my family arrived. At one point, twenty people must have been in the birthing room, celebrating the miracle of a biological mom and dad and the adoptive mom and dad coming together under God's infinitely wise best plan. The room was filled to overflowing with love, generosity, and the gift of a baby, our daughter.

We prayed with the social worker.

Bundled up Becca.

Placed her perfectly in the car seat.

Picked up the dog.

And we were off.

I remember thinking it was like a dream, but it wasn't *my* dream. It was *God's* dream for me, which is always so much better. I was walking in the path God had planned for me before the foundation of the world. He kindly whispered into my heart, *This is who I am—not as you think I should be but always for your good, Margo.*

> It was God's dream for me.

In adoptions, the biological parents have some allotted time to finalize the decision to terminate parental rights (TPR). This time completely depends on how quickly the courts are moving. Grandparents are also included in the agreement, mentioned as people who won't choose to try to raise the child. Until that paperwork came through and was approved in court, I chose to safely stay in God's waiting room.

But God had already prepared me for this emotional roller coaster, since I never knew, during my high-risk pregnancies, if I would continue to be pregnant the next day. He walked me through each day moment by moment and kept me choosing to stay focused on Him and not on my circumstances.

When we showed up in court, we didn't know whether the TPR agreement would be signed. By a miracle of God's timing and the courts moving quickly, the birth mother and father were already there. My sister and brother-in-law drove us. My mom came, too, but no one went into the court room with us. There were only Brian, me, the judge, and the biological parents. They immediately signed. They were smiling and grateful. (So were we!) We had small talk about how we promised to give Becca the best life ever.

The judge proclaimed the adoption final.

We received her forever-legal documents.

And took "happy tears" pictures together. Then our life began as Becca's mom and dad. We took our daughter home as though we had done so straight from the hospital.

The fact took a while to sink in that this was the child we had been praying and waiting for.

Through red-blotched faces, we cried, "Lord, thank You for this eternal soul on loan to us directly from You. In Your perfect time. In Your perfect way." We had Rebecca Elizabeth dedicated within a couple of months.

As our daughter, Becca, continued to grow, we began another adoption, this time internationally. Every day Becca prayed for a baby sister—so much so that she carried around her Bitty Baby doll everywhere she went.

This time God's timetable was a little longer, once again teaching me to wait and trust the unseen.

Our second little miracle, Tori, was born in Guatemala four years after Becca's birth. We learned she had been the seventh child born to the birth mother, after which time three of Tori's biological siblings had died of malnutrition before they reached the age of three. Our hearts were heavy. How do you handle that hard news? Needless to say, this adoption process had been arduous, really testing our faith.

Then my two favorite words, "but God," came into play once more. He was already on the scene at the embassy in Guatemala City before we ever showed up. There was a storm brewing in Guatemala, but Brian and I somehow walked through the country unscathed. In four days, we were headed home with our six-month-old bundle of joy strapped onto Daddy's chest.

She had the biggest dark-brown eyes you've ever seen. When we arrived home, we were greeted at the airport by over-the-top excited friends and family who had been praying for us every step of the way.

The best memory, however, was when we were coming down the plane's skyway. Our little four-year-old big sister, Becca, spotted us and bounded toward Brian and me. She jumped into my open right arm since baby Tori occupied my left arm. Thankfully, Brian steadied me, or we would have all toppled to the floor.

Now at eye level, Becca looked over at her new brown-skinned, brown-eyed Guatemalan sister and exclaimed, "Mom! Don't we look like twins?"

For just a moment, I looked at Becca's pearlescent skin, blue eyes, and white-blond hair alongside

Tori's brown skin, dark-brown eyes, and full head of gleaming black hair. I responded, "Yes, Becca. You do look like twins. When Jesus looks at Tori and you, He sees you just as you are."

Out of the mouths of babes—that's how Jesus sees all of us. "For God so loved the world [that's every color and ethnicity] that He gave His one and only Son, that whosoever [and we are all "whosoevers"] believes in Him shall not perish but have eternal life" (John 3:16 NIV, Margo revision).

> I imagine His delight as He saw me fully trust Him.

When I look back at God's amazing plan through the miracle of adoption, I imagine His delight as He saw me fully trust Him. The specifics—the who, what, when, why, and how of having a family—didn't matter anymore. I had gladly abandoned myself to His best plan in His time and His way. I continued to stay close enough to overhear His voice. That meant being in His Word.

Staying in His Word.

Praying His Word.

His Word became my very sustenance. Like Job, "I have not departed from the commands of His lips; I have treasured the words of His mouth more than my daily bread" (Job 23:12 NIV).

His desire is that I will trust the unseen, which allows me to "be anxious for nothing [not even how I am going to have kids], but in everything [which includes having a family] by prayer and supplication [petition, plea] with thanksgiving, let your requests [my heart thoughts] be made known to God; and the peace of God, which surpasses all understanding, will guard your hearts and minds through Christ Jesus" (Philippians 4:6–7 NKJV, Margo revision).

His Word is truer than true. He is an ever-present help in times of trouble. "Call upon Me in the day of trouble; I will deliver you, and you shall glorify me" (Psalm 50:15 NKJV).

That's just what I did. I gave Him all my days of trouble and saw His glory revealed. His fingerprints were written all over my life's circumstances.

When all I had was God, God was all I needed. Thanks, Corrie, for leading the way.

Lord, I praise You for bringing me to the end of myself. My wants. My desires. My timing. Forgive me for trying to play God. I did a miserable job of it. I'm so grateful You are the God who is enough. You are all I need. To think that You had my daughters picked out just for me before the foundation of the world—I fall on my face and can hardly utter a word. Even if I never would have had kids, I would still praise You since I know that I know You always have Your best plan. Tis so sweet to trust in Jesus. I will forever trust the unseen. I love You.

Devotions
for Your Next Right Steps

Always for My Good and His Glory

Just Do It!
More than Your Wildest Dreams
Rock-Solid Sure
No Embarrassment Here
You Have a Choice

Just Do It!

> My counsel for you is simple and straightforward: Just go ahead with what you've been given. You received Christ Jesus, the Master; now live him. You're deeply rooted in him. You're well constructed upon him. You know your way around the faith. Now do what you've been taught. School's out; quit studying the subject and start living it! And let your living spill over into thanksgiving.
>
> —Colossians 2:6–7 (MSG)

Why is it that, even though I *know* Jesus, I still don't step out on the water? Where is my absolute trust without borders? It seems all I have are calloused knees.

The apostle Paul's counsel is straightforward and simple: "Go ahead with what you have been given ... Jesus, the Master, now live Him!"

I have everything I need to live life to the full right now. What am I waiting for? I don't need to pray and pray and pray when I know the right thing to do. I just need to do it. Just do the next right thing.

"You're deeply rooted in Him. You're well-constructed upon Him. You know your way around the faith. Now do what you've been taught."

Remember being taught to read?

Now you can read.

Remember being taught to print the alphabet?
Now you can communicate by writing.
Remember being taught to type?
Now you're working on a laptop.
Or how about learning to play the piano?
Now you're making beautiful music.
Or being taught how to crochet?
Now you're making baby blankets for new arrivals.

Or being taught how to ski, throw a ball, ride a wakeboard, drive a car—the list could go on and on.

Well, because you were taught these activities, now you are using them. You are doing what you have been taught.

You don't keep studying books on how to do what you're doing and never put to use what you have learned. That would be foolish.

It's the same in our faith walk. We need to step out on the water, exercising our faith, so it will continue to grow stronger. If we never put what we have learned—God's promises—to the test, we will never really start living. Just go ahead and "be Jesus."

You have been studying Him, learning His ways. Now go ahead; do what you have been taught. "And let your living spill over into thanksgiving."

**Imitate Him in all you
think, speak, and do.**

More than Your Wildest Dreams

> God can do anything, you know—far more than you could ever imagine or guess or request in your wildest dreams! He does it not by pushing us around but by working within us, his Spirit deeply and gently within us. Glory to God in the church! Glory to God in the Messiah, in Jesus! Glory down all the generations! Glory through all millennia! Oh, yes!
>
> —Ephesians 3:20–21 (MSG)

Do you believe God can do anything? If not, you're having a crisis of belief.

He can do anything. He does do anything. He has done anything. He will do anything. The problem comes when I want Him to do "my thing" in "my timing" and in "my way."

So when you pray, when you ask Him to do _____ (fill in the blank), He has *the* best answer. Far more than you could ever imagine, guess, or request in your wildest dreams, He will do it.

Can He do anything? Oh yes! He is God. If His anything doesn't match "my thing," does that mean He hasn't answered or doesn't care?

Far from it! He has the best answer since He sees around corners before you're even there. He is answering you in a way that is for His glory.

Always for your good.

Always in His timing.

Always in His best way.

He answers so you can see His fingerprints all over your circumstances and burst out in grateful praise.

He does this by working within us, not by shoving us this way or that.

Not by pushing us over a cliff.

Not by ramming us through a doorway.

No. He speaks to us deeply and gently, telling us, "This is the way to go. Now walk in it."

Even when the walk looks scary? Yep. He already knows the way. All you need to do is hold onto His hand. Your Father won't take you anywhere He can't protect you.

He wants to show you His glory—His fingerprints—all over your situation. He has His absolute best for you right now and will do exceedingly abundantly more than you could ask, think, or imagine.

Your only concern is to trust, to listen and respond to His Spirit gently leading the way. Then you'll be able to see your circumstances through His eyes, and with a grateful voice, you'll proclaim, "Glory to God! Through all my days. Down through all the generations! Through all of eternity. Glory to God!"

Refocus.
Look at your circumstances
through His eyes.

Rock-Solid Sure

Because Jesus was raised from the dead, we've been given a brand-new life and have everything to live for, including a future in heaven—and the future starts now! I know how great this makes you feel, even though you have to put up with every kind of aggravation in the meantime. Pure gold put in the fire comes out of it proved pure; genuine faith put through this suffering comes out proved genuine. When Jesus wraps this all up, it's your faith, not your gold, that God will have on display as evidence of his victory.

—1 Peter 1:3–7 (MSG)

What do you keep on display? In a place of prominence? As a symbol of your accomplishment? Your graduation certificate from medical school? Your first blue ribbon at the county fair? A photo of you at the summit of Longs Peak? Or maybe it's that worn wedding ring you're wearing on your left hand?

Well, you know what God has framed, hanging up on His entrance wall for all to see? On display big-time? No, it's not a photo of you (even though He loves you very much). It's your faith.

Yep! Your faith is on display as evidence of His victory. Notice I said "His victory." Jesus has the victory all signed, sealed, and delivered.

He's yours for the believing.

He did it all.

He rose from the dead.

He gave you a brand-new life and everything to live for. He gave you a future in heaven, which starts now. All that's required is faith.

Hebrews 11:1 defines *faith* as "being certain of what you hope for and sure of what you do not see." So as you are walking through life and coming into a problem or coming out of a problem, you will still be "more than a conqueror" because you know that you know (that's faith) that God has allowed this circumstance for your good and His glory.

Your faith grows stronger only when it is tested, and it is tested so your faith will grow stronger. Then when the next storm comes, waves of doubt won't sweep you off to sea. No, you will be on the rock, so the waves will just wash over you. At the first drop of rain, you will begin to ask, "What do You want me to learn through this, Lord?"

Oh, what sweet victory!

Nothing in your circumstances has changed, but you have. Your faith is rock-solid sure in the Author and Finisher of your faith, Jesus. "Pure gold put in the fire comes out of it proved pure; genuine faith put through this suffering comes out proved genuine!" No wonder God has your faith on display.

**Your faith will be on display
as evidence of His victory.**

No Embarrassment Here

> If any of you are embarrassed over me and the way I'm leading you when you get around your fickle and unfocused friends, know that you'll be an even greater embarrassment to the Son of Man when he arrives in all the splendor of God, his Father, with an army of the holy angels.
>
> —Mark 8:38 (MSG)

Whoa!

Those are some powerful words from Jesus. But then again, why wouldn't they be? His words are to instruct, convict, exhort, and comfort. However, your relationship with Him will determine how you respond to His words.

Jesus made it clear that He and His leadership skills obviously embarrassed some of his followers. But not when they were with Him—only when they were around their fickle and unfocused friends. *Hmm.* That's rather hypocritical. They were acting one way when with the "religious" crowd and another when not.

Does that sound like anyone you know? I know there were times when it was me. I wanted Jesus to accept me so I could get all the benefits that go along with Him, like a home in heaven—but not so much of Jesus that I might have been counted as a "Jesus

Freak" or radical for Him. No, that would have been embarrassing.

Notice that Jesus didn't say that these fickle and unfocused friends are necessarily unbelievers. They seem to be up and down, riding their feelings instead of their faith. And He warned us not to be more concerned about what they are thinking than what He is thinking. He admonished us, saying that we should live before an audience of one—Him.

I'm grateful that I eventually recognized that a time could come, if I'd kept at my worldly ways, when Jesus would have been way more embarrassed of me than I was of Him. When He comes back in all His Father's splendor, with an army (that's a lot) of angels and all He has to offer, I want to share in His splendor, not be an embarrassment to Him. Therefore, I needed to stop feeling like He was an embarrassment to me.

> I want to share in His splendor, not be an embarrassment to Him.

Let Him lead.

He knows the way.

Just hold His hand.

Keep your eyes focused ahead on His path, with no chance for the fickle and unfocused friends to take over. No embarrassment can creep in then.

You know who's holding your hand.

You Have a Choice

> Don't love the world's ways. Don't love the world's goods. Love of the world squeezes out love for the Father. Practically everything that goes on in the world—wanting your own way, wanting everything for yourself, wanting to appear important—has nothing to do with the Father. It just isolates you from him. The world and all its wanting, wanting, wanting is on the way out—but whoever does what God wants is set for eternity.
>
> —1 John 2:15–17 (MSG)

There are only two ways to live: loving the world's ways and goods *or* loving the Father. They don't coexist. Loving the world will squeeze out your love for the Father. Period.

So, what or who are you loving more? When you're in His Word, you are being conformed to the likeness of His Son and His ways. And when you're in the world, you're being squeezed into its ways. You have a choice every moment of every day.

The key to loving the world is me oriented. My way. My selfish desires.

I'm-a-big-shot thinking.

If that's your mode of operations (MO), then you're well on your way to isolation from the heavenly Father.

That's not a good place to be. I'm sure it's not something you desire, but it will happen, since it has nothing to do with the Father and everything to do with promoting self.

That way of living—living for self—is on its way out. It can lead to temporary happiness, but it will only collapse in a heap.

A heap of regrets.

A heap of denials.

A heap of sorrow.

When we do what God wants us to do, we are set for eternity.

Then Jesus said to His disciples, "Whoever wants to be my disciple must deny themselves and take up their cross and follow me" (Matthew 16:24 NIV).

It's all about denying our own selfish ways and doing the next right thing. That's following Jesus. *That's* the key to loving the Father and not the world.

Following Jesus will make a difference now and for all eternity.

Chapter 7

Less like My Putrid Self

No perfect parents. No perfect kids. No perfect marriage.

Mom was right. Her words echoed in my heart. *God didn't put you in this marriage to make you happy. His ultimate purpose is to make you holy.*

Ugh. Really?

Coming home from a women's retreat, I was totally convicted. The minute I walked in the door, I asked my husband to sit on the couch so I could get on my knees and ask for forgiveness. I hadn't done anything morally wrong, but I sure was getting in the way of what God wanted to do in his life.

Actually, I was trying to be Brian's "convictor." I would make comments like "Did you see in the church bulletin? There's a men's small group starting up in our neighborhood." Or I'd accidentally (on purpose) leave the bulletin on his bedside table and circle when the next baptism service would be. I was trying to be Brian's personal Holy Spirit. Sigh.

He teared up. I wept. We prayed. God healed.

I had grown up in a family that was loud, laughing, gregarious, physical, and outgoing. Brian was more reserved and logical. He had been an only child in a multigenerational home, going to school in a one-room schoolhouse in a tiny town of less than one hundred people in northwestern Iowa. Those very different child-rearing years collide, even when you're one in Christ.

I could see God peeling back the layers in my husband's life—and mine. Thankfully, we were on the right path for us to individually and collectively grow up in Christ. He had learned relationship building through his fraternity years in college, while my parents had taught me that relationships were always more important than the tasks at hand.

I was a mover, and he was a processor. I didn't like the slower processing. I wanted everything talked about, and then we could move on. This was true in our marriage and in our walks with God.

Sadly, I kept focusing on how excellent Brian was in resolving conflict in the corporate world. But with me not so much. He could take a burning situation at work, douse the fire, and rebuild it into something that was better for everyone. I was so proud of him, but I wondered why he didn't do that on a personal level at home. He was amazing at that skill professionally, but it didn't necessarily follow through in our marriage. I wanted to talk through things and rectify it now rather than letting it fester until later. I had been taught that confrontation was a good thing. It was just *how* you walked through it that mattered. Plus, it wasn't as if Brian were living a wrong lifestyle. You could just see these two families colliding—one that fought through conflict and one that processed it slowly.

I had to learn that God had made us each unique, and that was another very good thing, not a bad thing.

The Holy Spirit was drawing Brian to Himself, and I needed to get out of the way. After all, I wasn't the "convictor"; God was—and is. So I released my honey to the one who loved him more than I could ever love him. I needed to let God be God.

Thirty years later, I still need to do the same thing, which allows me to be his helpmate and prayer warrior. (And that's a very good thing too.) It's a continual process of giving over the control to the one who is always in control.

> It's a continual process of giving over the control to the one who is always in control.

I realized there was enough yuck in my life that needed to be cleaned up before I saw Jesus face-to-face that I certainly didn't need to remind Brian of his shortcomings. It just seemed easier that way. Then I wouldn't have to work on my own issues.

However, as I allowed God to go to work on me, Brian completely surprised me and was baptized in the pond at church. He had a blast pulling that off. He invited friends and family for a picnic, and after the third service, on the grass knoll near the pond, he excused himself to use the facilities. The next thing I knew, he was down the hill, standing in line and waiting to be dunked.

It's so much better to "trust and obey," leaving all the consequences with God. (Thank you, Charles Stanley, for that morsel of wisdom.) There's another lesson learned.

The kids were growing like weeds by now. We were in the go-go-go years.

Go here.

Go there.

Go back to here.

We were running the kids to and from school, choir, soccer, cross-country, hip-hop praise, Awana, worship team, musicals, and training of our horse. Plus, by this time, I was an on-air radio personality, which meant I had to be at the station by four thirty for the *Morning Show* on 105.3 The Fish (today it's the Christian station K-LOVE). I now understood why my carpool van was a mom necessity. The vortex of family life was real. Days were filled with organized chaos. Isn't this what I had prayed for so many years ago?

I was learning to pray differently. I needed God's wisdom, and I needed it now. Thankfully, all I had to do was ask.

So I asked.

And asked.

And asked.

"If any of you lacks wisdom, you should ask God, who gives generously to all without finding fault, and it will be given to you" (James 1:5 NIV). God answered. He made more hours than there were in a day. He took things off my plate and put them on someone else's. He gave me wonderful, godly friends who helped shepherd my girls to school. Brian didn't travel as much for business.

The one nonnegotiable was my face-to-face time with Jesus. He centered me. He taught me how to parent and discipline according to each daughter's bent. He reminded me every day that I would never be the perfect wife or mom but definitely a forgiven one.

Seeing the girls blossom in beauty and stature made me burst with pride—not in a bad way but in the way that must make God beam when we are growing up in Him.

As the firstborn, Becca was an overachiever. Attending preschool at age two and a half, kindergarten, and then elementary grades, she skipped first grade—the little smarty-pants. After three years of middle school, eighth-grade graduation came—and zoom! High school arrived, which was full of expanding horizons. She loved participating in musicals, choir, Broadway choir, and state music competitions. Plus, she played on the soccer team, only to have both feet broken—and her dreams. But God's plans were way bigger. She took AP courses, was on National Honor Society, and enjoyed proms and homecomings with her boyfriend. Life was good, but before we knew it, we packed our Honda Pilot and U-Haul to the brim and moved our seventeen-year-old into her college dorm room. Yikes, that went fast.

Like any parent, I practiced on my first child, so I thought I was going to be pretty good on my second. Nothing could surprise me anymore—or so I thought.

Tori loved her big sister and wanted to be just like her. They played Barbie and Polly Pocket, by the hour. Their bedrooms spilled out into the upper hallway, which was filled with doll houses, doll furniture, doll cars, doll boats, doll wardrobes—doll everything. Oh, plus tons of Ken dolls and, of course, their babies.

Then there were VeggieTales and Donut Man videos, Steve Green cassette tapes and karaoke. They would sing in their frilly, pink dress-up clothes, perched on a homemade stage of steps in the sunroom. Brian and I listened while making sure to keep out of sight, giggling into our elbows.

Our second daughter was a charmer, a talker, and a social magnet. She was so petite; everyone was attracted to her. She was as smart as a whip in most classes and loved anything art. She excelled in cross-country and loved watching the Olympics, imagining she might be in the eight-hundred-meter relay someday.

By the time Tori was in middle school, we noticed she was becoming more and more rebellious. Troubling behaviors started to emerge. Before long, she had broken the law. We cried out to God, "Help. You have given us this precious child. Please rescue her."

Mercifully, He led us to have a neuropsychologist evaluate Tori, and the tests revealed she had a disorder called RAD (Reactive Attachment Disorder). To enjoy a "good" prognosis for life, she needed to have more structure than we were able to provide at home, and tomorrow couldn't be soon enough.

For many months, we had lived behind locked doors. We had prayed she wouldn't run away again or steal another iPhone, so God, as only He could do, opened a door to a Christian boarding school, and the judge granted us that decision. Praise God! The school provided the very structure Tori needed for a time, but soon that school wasn't structured enough. We went through years of finding the right schools and the help our daughter needed.

> For many months, we had lived behind locked doors.

Tribulation.

Desperation.

Perseverance.
Character.
Hope.
And hope doesn't disappoint.

God heard and answered. "And not only that, but we also glory in tribulations, knowing that tribulation produces perseverance; and perseverance, character; and character, hope. Now hope does not disappoint, because the love of God has been poured out in our hearts by the Holy Spirit who was given to us" (Romans 5:3–5 NKJV).

As I walked through each moment, holding tightly to His hand, not only was my God-given daughter going to be changed forever, but I was too. I'm pretty sure I expected to have perfect daughters, since I had gone through so much trouble to even be able to have children.

After all, look at what I had gone through! Me! Me! Me!

I had copped a how-did-this-affect-me attitude. Ouch. God was peeling back my onion skin and revealing quite the stench underneath.

He graciously used this desperate situation—not only for the hope of Tori's eventual

> I needed to become more and more like Jesus and less and less like my putrid self.

healing but for mine as well. I needed to become more and more like Jesus and less and less like my putrid self. He was actively pruning me again. I realized there was no treading water with Jesus. I was either going to exhibit forward progress with Him at the lead or backward momentum, prompted by my own stubborn ways. I chose to let Him lead. "Every branch in Me that does not bear fruit, He takes away; and every branch that continues to bear fruit, He [repeatedly] prunes, so that it will bear more fruit [even richer and finer fruit]" (John 15:2 AMP).

That's what He was doing—pruning so there would be less of me and more of Him. Oh, it was so very hard, but I will never regret how God surgically went to work on me ever so tenderly. He cut away my mommy's dreams and replaced them with His *big* dreams for both of my daughters.

After all, He sweetly reminded me, *your children are Mine. I see them. I created Becca and Tori in My image. They are just on loan to you.*

Gratefully, I began to change my focus from the how-does-this-affect-me mentality to *What are You trying to teach me through this, Lord?*

That was my turning point of becoming more and more like Him and less like my putrid self.

Oh, God, forgive me for my self-righteousness. My heart weeps for all the years I wasted, but I know that I know your Word says, "You give back all the years the locusts have eaten." Nothing is wasted. You always use it somehow in some way for my good and Your glory. I am overwhelmed with Your unconditional love, a love that "covers a multitude of sin." My sin. Help me to be filled to overflowing with Your love. Keep me becoming more and more like You, whatever it takes. I give You full permission to have Your way with me.

**Devotions
for Your Next Right Steps**

God's Purifying Process

Meant for So Much More
Count on It!
Get Dressed
Bright Morning Light
Brand-New Threads

Meant for So Much More

> Listen carefully: Unless a grain of wheat is buried in the ground, dead to the world, it is never any more than a grain of wheat. But if it is buried, it sprouts and reproduces itself many times over. In the same way, anyone who holds on to life just as it is, destroys that life. But if you let it go, reckless in your love, you'll have it forever, real and eternal. If any of you wants to serve me, then follow me. Then you'll be where I am, ready to serve at a moment's notice. The Father will honor and reward anyone who serves me.
>
> —John 12:24–26 (MSG)

Jesus shared a practical story with a deeper meaning so we could understand more fully how to follow Him. He always gave us analogies and parables so our small minds could understand His big truths.

> The grain has to be willing to die to itself.

He started off with a farming example and turned it into life-giving advice.

A grain of wheat is just that, a grain of wheat. It won't become a bushel of wheat unless it's planted deep underground, dead to the world, where it will sprout and reproduce itself many times over.

No one is able to be nourished from one grain of wheat. But a bushel of wheat? That's another story. There's plenty for you and your family, plus others in need in your neighborhood.

But the grain has to be willing to die to itself underground so it can sprout and be reproduced. Then it is useful. Then it is fulfilling its original potential.

See, the grain of wheat was always meant for more. The potential for it to be reproduced many times over already existed in itself, but it would take dying to self to reach its full potential.

Jesus said the truth is the same with us. It's when we die to ourselves—

> Our wants,
>   Our ways,
>   Our plans,
>   Our interests

—that we sprout. Instead of being consumed with me, me, me (the trinity of me), it becomes all about Thee, Thee, Thee.

> Your ways,
>   Your wants,
>   Your plans,
>   Your interests.

The focus is off me and on Thee.

That's reckless love. It's when you give away your life that you truly find it. You've gone from a measly piece of grain to a useful, overflowing bushel. That's God's economy. Multiplication through death. It's then that you experience real life—and forever.

Plus, you will be honored and rewarded by the heavenly Father as you follow His Son. Where He is you will be at His side. What He does you will do. Where He goes you will go. What He says you will say.

Remember, you have died to your old ways, plans, and language.

**You are sprouting and
reproducing not you but Him.**

Count On It!

Because Jesus was raised from the dead, we've been given a brand-new life and have everything to live for, including a future in heaven—and the future starts now! God is keeping careful watch over us and the future. The Day is coming when you'll have it all—life healed and whole. I know how great this makes you feel, even though you have to put up with every kind of aggravation in the meantime. Pure gold put in the fire comes out of it proved pure; genuine faith put through this suffering comes out proved genuine. When Jesus wraps this all up, it's your faith, not your gold, that God will have on display as evidence of his victory.

—1 Peter 1:3–7 (MSG)

What a victorious thought! "We've been given a brand, new life and have everything to live for, including a future in heaven!" And it's not just wishful thinking. It's truth. Because Jesus was raised from the dead, we can count on it starting right now.

We have everything to live for now on this side of heaven. We don't need to wait until we move to heaven. Your brand-new life started when you accepted Jesus as your Savior. And yes, you have heaven in your future—guaranteed. But now is when you start really living.

Oh, there are going to be aggravations in this old, fallen world. Jesus even told us in John 16:33 (NIV), "In this world, you will have trouble. But take heart! I have overcome the world." So even when life's yuck comes along, we have no excuse. He has already paved the way for us to lead a whole and healed life now.

But what does it require to live a victorious life now?

Money? Fame? Education? No. It requires only faith. Yep, that's it. Faith in the one true God, who is "keeping careful watch over us and the future."

Living a victorious life now takes nothing we can earn on our own and everything Jesus already accomplished for us on the cross because He's not still on the cross. He defeated death and the grave so we can live the abundant life in Him now and forever in heaven. "When you were stuck in your old sin-dead life, you were incapable of responding to God. God brought you alive—right along with Christ! Think of it! All sins forgiven, the slate wiped clean, that old arrest warrant canceled and nailed to Christ's cross. He stripped all the spiritual tyrants in the universe of their sham authority at the Cross and marched them naked on the streets" (Colossians 2:13–15 MSG). We can live our victorious life now because of Jesus's victory over death. All it requires is faith.

> Living a victorious life now takes nothing we can earn on our own.

**Live the abundant life in Him now
and forever. You can count on it!**

Get Dressed

The night is about over, dawn is about to break. Be up and awake to what God is doing! God is putting the finishing touches on the salvation work he began when we first believed. We can't afford to waste a minute, must not squander these precious daylight hours in frivolity and indulgence, in sleeping around and dissipation, in bickering and grabbing everything in sight. Get out of bed and get dressed! Don't loiter and linger, waiting until the very last minute. Dress yourselves in Christ, and be up and about!

—Romans 13:12–14 (MSG)

Have you ever been awake at the coming of the dawn, anticipating the light that will flood the earth? Darkness cannot coexist with light. Neither can it coexist in those who are followers of Jesus.

If you want to see the coming of the dawn, you need to be up so you can experience the light pushing back the darkness. That's what light does. Darkness has to obey light.

> Darkness has to obey the light.

So get up. Be awake. Observe what God is doing. You will miss out on the finishing touches He wants to accomplish in and through you if you just sleepwalk through the dark. No frivolous stuff. No indulging. No sleeping around. No dissipation. No bickering. No grabbing everything in sight. Stay away from that dark stuff.

Live in the light since He *is* light.

Since your day of salvation, your day of believing and receiving Jesus as your Savior, He is continuing to refine you. He lives in you; therefore, you are filled with light.

Do the next right thing.

Get up. Get out of bed, feet to the floor. Don't just lollygag around. Get going. No loitering. No waiting to get dressed at the last minute before you need to be somewhere. Report for duty. But first you need to get dressed in Christ so you will look just like Him. Then as you are up and about for the day, your clothes will shine.

Others will see Jesus's light in you.

Bright Morning Light

> Let the morning bring me word of your unfailing love, for I have put my trust in you. Show me the way I should go, for to you I entrust my life. Teach me to do your will, for you are my God; may your good Spirit lead me on level ground.
>
> —Psalm 143:8,10 (NIV)

Are you a morning person? It's the breaking of a new day, the dawn arising, a new beginning once again.

The ultimate redo. Start over. Clean slate.

It's in the light that you can see clearly. Dawn has pushed back darkness. In fact, darkness *has* to obey light. Just walk into a dark room and shine a flashlight, maybe a candle or even just a match. Darkness flees for even the smallest bit of light.

No wonder the psalmist wrote, "Let the morning bring me word of your unfailing love." He was counting on the new day, knowing that whatever happened (his circumstances), He would trust in God's unfailing love.

Lamentations 3:22–23 (NKJV) points out that "through the Lord's mercies we are not consumed, Because His compassions fail not. They are new every morning; Great is Your faithfulness." When you rise with God in the morning, He clearly illuminates the way. In the night, you can't see as clearly, but know that if you can just hold on until the morning light, God will direct your path.

Notice that even in the dark, the psalmist trusted the one who could see. He had already recklessly abandoned himself to Him. He trusted God in the dark, knowing that in the morning he would see what he previously could not: "the way he should go." There were many ways he *could* go, but he wanted the right path, so he waited on God to show him.

Waiting.

Expectantly waiting.

Waiting expectantly is about knowing (that you know) that God, through the Holy Spirit, will lead you on level ground. If you take off on your own, you'll be trudging up mountains, falling into deep crevasses, and walking on paths full of potholes and uneven terrain in the dark.

God wants to lead you on level ground in the light. Even if the mountains loom on the horizon, He will have you walk on level ground around them or through them as He levels the path along the way.

Just trust Him—His unfailing love, His way, His will. For He is *my* God, and I entrust my life to Him.

Teach me to do Your will.
Show me the way to go.

Brand-New Threads

Don't lie to one another. You're done with that old life. It's like a filthy set of ill-fitting clothes you've stripped off and put in the fire. Now you're dressed in a new wardrobe. Every item of your new way of life is custom-made by the Creator, with His label on it ... So, chosen by God for this new life of love, dress in the wardrobe God picked out for you: compassion, kindness, humility, quiet strength, discipline. Be even-tempered, content with second place, quick to forgive an offense. Forgive as quickly and completely as the Master forgave you. And regardless of what else you put on, wear love. It's your basic, all-purpose garment. Never be without it.

—Colossians 3:9–10, 13–14 (MSG)

Look in your closet. Do you still have old, ill-fitting clothes that should be removed? They're useless, taking up space, perhaps reminding you of your old life, your old ways. Get rid of them.

You'll want to have plenty of room for your new wardrobe. And who doesn't like that? Garments custom-made for you, tailored to fit you perfectly. Designer labels. Oh, not just any designer. Thee

Designer! You'll be dressed in a new wardrobe, custom made with His label on it.

But here's the deal: you need to get rid of the old clothes before you can put on "His label" finery. God has picked out your wardrobe. Dress in compassion. Clothe yourself in kindness, humility, and discipline. Wear quiet strength. These basics will never wear out, never go out of style. And as the final touch to your outfit, put on love. It's your all-purpose garment. Never be without it.

God's picked out His wardrobe just for you so you could look just like Him. That's more than looking like a million bucks. Others will compliment your complete look. Your response? "It's the latest style now and forever. It's called 'His label.'"

**He's got an ensemble
picked out perfectly for you, too.**

Chapter 8

I *Am* Fit

Walking. Walking no matter what. Walking in winter, spring, summer, and fall.

If I hadn't been spiritually fit during the waiting-for-the-other-shoe-to-drop years, I would have missed out on God's unexpected blessings.

Amid the trials.

In the heat of uncertainties.

Always with the promises of His Word.

I kept walking.

After all, He cannot deny Himself.

"This is a faithful saying: For if we die with Him, we shall also live with Him. If we endure, we shall also reign with Him. If we deny Him, He will also deny us. If we are faithless, He remains faithful; He cannot deny Himself" (2 Timothy 2:11–13 NKJV).

Eugene H. Peterson authored *A Long Obedience in the Same Direction*, which became a useful weapon in my arsenal of tools for keeping spiritually fit. I didn't just settle for salvation through Jesus, but I followed hard after Him. I had become a disciple of Jesus Christ. I knew my only hope was in my Savior. I had spent the time and energy to get to know Him and His ways, returning to my life verse time and time again. "I want to know Christ and the power of His resurrection and the fellowship of sharing in His sufferings" (Philippians 3:10 NIV).

Christ followers are made for tough times. As I fought the thought battle during times of trouble, I'd run to my Refuge, my Strength, and my ever-present Help. And there I would stay.

Such purpose.

Such hope.

"Hope means a confident, alert expectation that God will do what He said He will do. It is imagination put in the harness of faith. It is a willingness to let God do it His way and in His time. It is the opposite of making plans that demand that God put into effect, telling him both how and when to do it. That is not hoping in God but bullying God" (Eugene H. Peterson, *A Long Obedience in the Same Direction: Discipleship in an Instant Society*).

> Unexpected, erratic waves of guilt, doubt, and fear would rage against me.

As well-meaning Christians talked behind my back, whispering, "Did you know Margo Fieseler sent her daughter away to a Christian boarding school? I mean, Margo Fieseler! What kind of a mother does that?" I had to immediately give the hurt over to the one who knows hurt.

I cried out to heaven, "Father, forgive them. They know not what they do." (Those were some of Jesus's last words on the cross as a legalistic, religious mob crucified him.)

Unexpected, erratic waves of guilt, doubt, and fear would rage against me as I crept through the boarding school's factual reports of Tori's inexcusable behavior. Whenever my phone rang, my racing heart and sweaty palms became the norm. *But God!* His powerful Word drowned out the enemy as I boldly spoke Psalm 112:7 before I picked up the phone. "They do not fear bad news; they confidently trust the Lord to care for them." And then this verse became personally mine:

> I do not fear bad news.
> I confidently trust the Lord
> to care for me
> and to care for Tori.

Moses became my hero. I hung onto his Red Sea moment from Exodus 14 while my Tori was in her own exodus from me. He had led the Israelites out of slavery in Egypt, through the desert, and to the shore of the Red Sea, which was lapping at his feet. The Israelites were still grumbling. Plus, six hundred Egyptian chariots, horses, horsemen, and troops were pursuing them.

Though no one else seemed to be spiritually fit, it took only one.

There Moses stood.

The Red Sea before him.

The terrified Israelites behind him.

The ground beneath their sandaled feet rumbled as the Egyptian army swiftly approached.

Not a good situation to be in.

Seemingly, no way out.

Unwavering

But God! (There are my two favorite words again.) Spiritually fit Moses turned to his people and proclaimed, "Do not be afraid. Stand firm, and you will see the deliverance the Lord will bring you today. The Egyptians you see today you will never see again. The Lord will fight for you; you need only to be still" (Exodus 14:13–14 NIV).

Wow, Moses. Just wow. (I can hardly wait to meet him when I move to heaven some glorious day.) Moses knew God. I mean, he *knew* God. And God knew Moses. Moses had followed hard after God, so when life hit him upside the head (as my mom might say), what was already inside spilled out.

Faith.
Confidence.
Assurance.
Compassion.
Wisdom.
Leadership.
Boldness.
Humility.
Power.

We all know the end of this story, don't we? But Moses had no idea what God was going to do—only that He *knew* God. He trusted in the great I Am, and that's all that mattered.

Moses was already delivered in or out of the "Nightmare at the Red Sea." Either way, he was delivered. Before Moses needed God to be his deliverer, He had gotten to know God, the Deliverer.

Me too. There was no need to be overwhelmed
By the unknown,
By the uncertainties,
By the next bad-news scenario.

God would deliver me (and Tori) in or out of our own "Red Sea nightmare." Either way, we would be delivered.

I needed to keep spiritually fit so when troubles rolled in (anytime of the day or night), I rolled them onto Jesus. They certainly didn't take *Him* by surprise.

An unexpected blessing during those turbulent years was that I learned to turn to God first. That was a big deal for me, since I had been going to my posse of girlfriends first and then tagging on prayer last. How sad is that? I thought I would figure it all out in my peanut, finite mind and then ask the God of all to bless my idea. It was totally twisted thinking.

> I needed to keep spiritually fit.

In my desperation, God taught me to pray in an unexpected way. I didn't ask Him, "Teach me to pray." I just called out to Him as I was walking—literally walking—four miles a day through neighborhoods, parks, preserves, and around the lake. I was cruising through a pair of trail walkers every three months.

I felt such exhilaration just to walk and talk with my best friend, Jesus. Plus, my favorite furry friend, Willow Joy, was by my side. (At times, my collie wanted to quit before I did. We had a come-to-Jesus talk about that.) Not only was I staying spiritually fit, but I was becoming more and more physically fit. It was a wonderful side benefit.

My walks turned into prayer walks. I couldn't help but praise Him as God's creation shouted aloud. The herons, sandhill cranes, turkeys, white-tailed deer, friendly dogs, and not-so-friendly dogs surrounded me. It was as if I were St. Francis of Assisi, the patron saint of animals. Chirps of robins, tweets of goldfinches, caws of crows, shrieks of blackbirds, shrills of cardinals, and the familiar call of the red-winged blackbird (my favorite) were singing His praises, and I was privileged to overhear their choir.

How could I not praise the God of all creation? Praise erupted from my soul onto my lips. Prayer was as natural as breathing. I had never experienced communing with almighty God this intimately. Even if my circumstances never changed, I knew the one who would carry me through safely to the other side. Oswald Chambers, author of the classic devotional *My Utmost for His Highest*, wrote, "Prayer does not fit us for the greater work: prayer *is* the greater work."

As my prayer life grew deeper, so did my relationship with Jesus. Prayer wasn't just an obligatory duty three times per day or only something to say as grace at dinnertime. I knew I was being ushered into His presence, which at times allowed a quiet hush, where we would converse. Instead of always babbling away, telling Him all my woes, there was comfort in the silence I shared with Him.

When you get to a point in your life where "God is all you have, God is all you need" (Corrie ten Boom), I think you also get to the point of fully and recklessly abandoning your life—your all—to Him.

All your desires.

All your expectations.

All your days.

You learn to trust Him like you trust the physical properties of water, knowing water will hold you up if you just remain still, but if you flail, you begin to drown. Its innate buoyancy will keep you afloat. It *has* to. It was designed for that. Water can't do anything else but keep you from sinking—*if* you let it. That's what I learned as I kept crying out to God, "I *know* You are my Refuge, my ever-present Help in times of trouble. You can't be anything else but that! That's *who* You are, not just what You do. I know that I know!"

That "know" is continual—not only walking and praying but also listening, steeping in God's Word, and purposely placing His truth into my heart. So when He tells me to "be anxious for nothing," I'm not to fill that "nothing" in with "something." I would acknowledge, "Lord, I'm anxious for this or that. I desire to be anxious for nothing. I'm giving that over to You."

I chose to let the God of all comfort hold me up. After all, He is the Living Water.

I also noticed that if I prayed aloud, all my other thought processes were at bay because I was thinking, saying, and hearing the prayer just as if I were conversing with a friend. It is a good habit that keeps my mind from being distracted. Plus, when I walked and talked in God's glorious creation, I was also physically motivated, since exercising releases those chemicals called endorphins that trigger a positive feeling in the body.

> If I prayed aloud, all my other thought processes were at bay.

I practiced praying scripture on my daily four-mile jaunts. When God has spoken (His Word) and you are agreeing with Him, you know that you know He has it already done in the heavens. Those are His promises, and He can't be anything but faithful. He's God. I learned to expectantly wait on Him to reveal the "how" and "when."

His timing.

His way.

His best for me.

I learned to let His Word speak truth into my heart. It was a balm for my soul. I clung to His every promise as if my life depended on it. My prayers became a cycle of listening and speaking, weeping for joy and sorrow, and tenderly healing my broken heart. He promises to "draw near to you as you draw near to Him" (James 4:8), and I wanted to be His intimate. I not only wanted but also needed to be His intimate. I remember Mom sharing that she never wanted to be more than two inches from the cross. Prayer kept me close to the cross.

In the middle of praying for my daughter, I was reminded of a time when I had needed prayer as a daughter. While working at 105.3 The Fish radio station, I looked forward to calling my mom every day after I was off the air. We'd pour into each other, sharing the highlights and the not-so highlights of the day and taking them to His throne together.

This particular day had been a really, really hard day. Everything that could go wrong did. The tech went down, the tower had troubles, my pull-out keyboard fell down and landed on my toe, my document didn't save, and I had to write last-minute scripts for on-air clients. I'd been there since four thirty in the morning until after six o'clock that night.

As I walked to my van, I gave Mom a call. After all, her number was on speed dial, and I could hardly wait to chat. Then it hit me—she had died several months earlier.

I remembered lying next to mom's bedside as she moved to heaven. She lovingly raised her finger toward me in a knowing sort of way and softly whispered, "Margo, you be faithful."

I said, "I will, Mom. I will. Until I see you face-to-face again."

Clinging onto those last words and missing her voice after that hard day as I drove home, I was weeping buckets, even heaving. I should have pulled over. I was screaming at God at the top of my lungs.

"It's not okay that my mom's dead right now! It's not okay. I need to talk to my mom. I know You're the God who can do anything, and I want to talk to her for ten minutes. I don't know how, but I want to talk to her."

I drove the forty-five minutes home, ranting at God the whole way. I walked into the utility room in the house and lay on the dryer, covered in the aftermath of ugly crying.

My girls ran to me and asked, "Mom, are you okay?"

We talked; they reminded me that "Nana" was with Jesus, and I said I knew that, but I just wanted to talk with her for ten minutes. Becca lovingly stroked my arm while Tori in her compassionate way brought me every collie stuffed animal she could find. Brian came home from work and walked into this confusing scene.

"Dad, Mom said it's not okay that Nana is dead."

"It's *not* okay," I said to Brian. "I know He's the God who is enough, and I know Mom would never want to leave Him. I know she's with Jesus—I know. But I also know I can talk to her because He's the God of the impossible."

"Okay," I said to God, "Four minutes. I know I can reason with You, so I'm asking for four minutes instead of ten."

I continued to wait for an answer while the music played in the background at home. Selah's song "Press On" came on. I became very still. A complete calm came over me, and I absorbed every note and lyric. It was as if time stood still.

> When the valley is deep
> When the mountain is steep
> When the body is weary
> When we stumble and fall

When it came to the chorus, I listened even more intently.

> In Jesus' name, we press on
> Dear Lord, with the prize
> Clear before our eyes
> We find the strength to press on.

I knew we owned the compact disc with that song, so I asked one of my daughters, "Would you go and check that song on the disc? How long is it?"

It was four minutes exactly. As a radio girl, I knew an exactly even time on a song was unique. What's more is that I knew those lyrics were just what Mom would have told me. *Margo, press on. In Jesus, you find the strength to press on.*

(How incredibly intimate and sweet for God to use Selah since they were Mom's favorite group, too.) God gave me my four minutes with Mom. And a God who could give me four minutes with my dead mother could certainly give me miracles in the lives of my living daughters.

Thank You, God. Even when I scream at You, You still mercifully give me the desire of my heart.

Our God is a big, big God. He can take your screaming and yelling. He wants you to be honest with yourself—and with Him—since He already knows your thoughts and feelings. Holding back is just keeping out the oneness you can have in your personal and private conversations with Him.

God became my Comforter, my Counselor, and my "Convictor"! I was an overcomer despite the uncertainties of life. The great I Am had gone before me. He was making every crooked path straight. I was to keep walking, trusting, waiting, praying, and reading His guidebook. After all, it has everything I need for life and godliness. "His divine power has given us everything we need for a godly life through our knowledge of Him who called us by his own glory and goodness" (2 Peter 1:3 NIV).

I had learned the equation for keeping spiritually fit: an ongoing process of pursuing the one who had pursued me.

Lord, let me never look back except to see how faithful You have always been. When I was trembling and afraid, You comforted me. When I was hurting beyond belief, You tenderly counseled me. When I wanted to throw in the towel, You convicted me to do the next right thing. You are always the answer. You are my remedy for whatever is ailing me. Help me to keep my eyes on You alone and off the Red Sea moments lapping at my feet. I know that I know You will continually make a way as I trust You with unwavering faith.

Devotions
for Your Next Right Steps

I'm an Overcomer

God Confidence
Spiritual Fitness
Right Word at the Right Time
A New Personal Record
Be Anxious for Nothing

God Confidence

> Don't be so naive and self-confident. You're not exempt. You could fall flat on your face as easily as anyone else. Forget about self-confidence; it's useless. Cultivate God-confidence. No test or temptation that comes your way is beyond the course of what others have had to face. All you need to remember is that God will never let you down; he'll never let you be pushed past your limit; he'll always be there to help you come through it.
>
> —1 Corinthians 10:12–13 (MSG)

Who do you place your confidence in? Who do you depend on? The government? Your employer? Your pastor? Yourself?

You are setting yourself up for disappointment and defeat if you place your confidence in anything or anyone other than God. "Don't be so naive and self-confident. You're not exempt. You could fall flat on your face as easily as anyone else." Ouch! I've literally fallen flat on my face before. Once it was on the ice. It required ten stitches. And a bruised ego. Not a good place to be.

The apostle Paul advised us to "forget about self-confidence; it's useless." We need Someone bigger and wiser who knows the end from the beginning, who sees the big picture and not just the little snapshot of life we are currently standing in.

And who is that Someone? God! The omnipotent (all-powerful), omnipresent (everywhere-present), and omniscient (all-knowing) God. Instead of depending on yourself, you're supposed to cultivate God confidence. Depend on Him. Trust Him. He sure has the right credentials.

Cultivate means "to promote or improve the growth [in God], by labor and attention." So as you cultivate God confidence, you need to be intentional. It takes work and attention to His ways, thoughts, and direction. And all those would be housed in God's Word, the BIBLE (or those Basic Instructions Before Leaving Earth).

Then, when a test or temptation pops up, you will be ready. You have cultivated God confidence. You know that you know He will never let you down. He will never let you be pushed past your limit. He will take you through it. You can be sure. You have been attentive to Him.

**Cultivate your God confidence
to see you through the trial.**

Spiritual Fitness

> Exercise daily in God—no spiritual flabbiness, please! Workouts in the gymnasium are useful, but a disciplined life in God is far more so, making you fit both today and forever. You can count on this. Take it to heart.
>
> —1 Timothy 4:8–10 (MSG)

Physical exercise is a good thing to help you *get* in shape and *stay* there. It keeps the extra pounds and flabbiness away. It combats health conditions and diseases. Plus, it improves your moods, boosts your confidence, and raises your self-esteem. You'll have more energy during the day and deeper sleep at night. Daily exercise seems like a no-brainer with all these life-giving benefits.

It doesn't help much, however, if you exercise one day and never move a foot or finger the other six days. You must be disciplined daily to gain the rewards of physical exercise, and that discipline pays off.

Days turn into weeks.

Weeks turn into months.

Months turn into years.

Pretty soon this exercise thing isn't something you do; it's who you are. It's part of you. Your lifestyle. You can't imagine a day without some sort of running, walking, circuit training, lifting weights, or whatever it is that gets you motivated to be physically fit.

Physical training and exertion help keep you fit right now on this earth. But what about being fit forever? That requires a different kind of workout. Instead of doing crunches, the elliptical, or running, you must exercise spiritually.

Exercise daily in God. Exercising in God also demands discipline. Specifically, you need nonnegotiable, face-to-face time with Jesus every day.

> Exercising in God also demands discipline.

Open His Word.

Get out your journal.

Earnestly pray, maybe even on your knees.

Listen.

Respond.

As the days, weeks, months, and years go by, you'll be spiritually in shape. You'll become more and more like Jesus and less like your putrid self. Just as your physical flabbiness gets toned up, so will your spiritual fleshiness. You can count on it. Keep on exercising. The dividends are for all eternity.

**God is making you fit
both today and forever.**

Right Word at the Right Time

> A bit in the mouth of a horse controls the whole horse. A small rudder on a huge ship in the hands of a skilled captain sets a course in the face of the strongest winds. A word out of your mouth may seem of no account, but it can accomplish nearly anything—or destroy it! It only takes a spark, remember, to set off a forest fire. A careless or wrongly placed word out of your mouth can do that. By our speech we can ruin the world, turn harmony to chaos, throw mud on a reputation, send the whole world up in smoke and go up in smoke with it, smoke right from the pit of hell.
>
> —James 3:3–6 (MSG)

Words. We use them every day. It's the major way we communicate with each other either for good or not so much.

How would you be remembered for your mouth? Encouraging? Edifying? Or for gossip? Idle talk? Coarse joking?

Well, James told us that your tongue is a small part of your whole body, just like a bit in a horse's mouth or a rudder on a ship. But it controls your whole body, just like a bit controls the whole horse and the rudder sets the ship on course.

So you need to be very careful what you say since there is death and life in the power of your tongue.

A little word from you can change someone's life. It can be a right word at the right time or a word of destruction.

> A little word from you can change someone's life.

That old saying "Sticks and stones may break my bones but words will never hurt me" isn't true. A careless word is compared to a little spark from a fire. It doesn't seem like it could do much, but it can and does. It can set off a whole forest fire. What devastation!

Our speech reflects who we are and has a lot to say about us and our character. So if you know your speech can ruin the world, create chaos, puke all over someone's reputation, and basically send your life up in smoke, that truth should be pretty concerning to you.

How can we take control over our tongues? Well, we can't. We have to surrender our speech to the Author of speech, to the Creator of our tongues. After all, "what you say flows from what is in your heart" (Luke 6:45 NLT).

As we are changed on the inside, what will flow out of our mouths will reflect our regenerated heart.

Remember, when life bumps into you, what's already on the inside is what spills out.

A changed heart will produce a changed mouth.

A New Personal Record

> I'm not saying that I have this all together, that I have it made. But I am well on my way, reaching out for Christ, who has so wondrously reached out for me. Friends, don't get me wrong: By no means do I count myself an expert in all of this, but I've got my eye on the goal, where God is beckoning us onward—to Jesus. I'm off and running, and I'm not turning back.
>
> —Philippians 3:12–14 (MSG)

What are you running toward? What goal do you have your eyes on? We are all running toward something. A promotion? Losing those last ten pounds? (Ugh!) More money for your retirement years in your 401(k)?

Those are all worthwhile goals, but the apostle Paul reminded us to have *one* goal in life and never to stop moving toward it.

Sometimes jogging.

Sometimes walking.

Sometimes crawling.

But we should always be moving forward, reaching out for Jesus, who has already reached out for us.

That's it! That's our one goal.

To know Jesus personally, passionately, powerfully, and preeminently. All the other goals will flow out of that one.

It's not that we have already attained that goal, but we are well on our way. Jesus already made it possible through the cross for us to have a personal relationship with God the Father. So now we can take off running, holding onto His hand, and never turning back.

That way we won't lag behind, run ahead, or fall flat on our faces. As we hold His hand, our one goal of knowing Him grows deeper. We've gone from knowing Him personally to knowing Him passionately. Our hearts leap at the sound of His name. We want what He wants. Our desire is to please Him.

> You realize, as you are running with Him, that He is your strength.

Then we realize, as we are running with Him, that He *is* our strength. Supernatural strength. We can run hills like never before. In fact, we have a new personal record. We are now knowing Him powerfully.

And as we keep putting one foot in front of the other, we notice our feet keep in step with His. He becomes preeminent over each step, each decision, each detail. That means He rules over our finances. Over our careers. Over our personal health. Over our families. Over our marriages. And over those other life goals? They now flow out of our *one major goal*—to know Jesus PPPP.

Personally.
Passionately.
Powerfully.
Preeminently.

Be Anxious for Nothing

> Don't fret or worry. Instead of worrying, pray. Let petitions and praises shape your worries into prayers, letting God know your concerns. Before you know it, a sense of God's wholeness, everything coming together for good, will come and settle you down. It's wonderful what happens when Christ displaces worry at the center of your life.
>
> —Philippians 4:6–7 (MSG)

Are you a worrywart? Did you know God didn't create you to worry? Instead, He created you as a dependent creature on Him.

The one who knows the end from the beginning.

The omniscient one.

The one who is in control.

He wants you to hold His hand as you cross the busy street of life. He will order your steps. Remember, Proverbs 16:9 says, "Man plans his way, *but God directs his steps*" (emphasis mine).

That verse should put a smile on your face. A skip in your step.

It means you need to purpose in your heart to trust Him, the God who sees. Trust your unseen future to the one who already knows it. That seems simple enough, doesn't it? Then why don't we do it? Why do we live anxiously about all the what-ifs?

We have a propensity to live our days independently of God, thinking we can handle whatever comes along, thinking we're the "gods" of our lives. Conveniently leaving God out of the equation until we come to a place where we feel out of control.

Your husband just lost his job. Your daughter has been diagnosed with a rare disease. Your mom needs to move into assisted living. Your finances are in shambles. Your oldest is headed off to college. You have feelings that you're in over your head. Quite frankly, you're overwhelmed with life.

> Stop the downward spiral of worry and let God know your concerns.

Where do you turn for help? For guidance? For wisdom? For your sanity? Fret and worry haven't been working for you (and never will). God is waiting for you to look up instead of continuing on in your eddy current of worry.

Pray! Stop the downward spiral of worry and let God know your concerns. He's wondering what took you so long to turn to Him. He's always at the ready to listen to your petitions and to respond with the best solution.

> He made you to be in an abiding relationship with Him.

Then you will have peace. Peace that will guard your heart and mind. Interminable peace. You will realize that everything is coming together for the good. Not that all your circumstances are good, but they will somehow and in some way work out for your good and His glory.

Run to Him. Keep yourself on a short leash. Tell Him all your concerns, joys, troubles, and sorrows. He has a sweet, attentive ear and already knows what is best for you.

He made you to be in an abiding relationship with Him. When you step away and do your own thing, worry will accompany you. And it's not very good company. Worry will tear you apart and spit you out for dinner. That's not God's intention.

Pray.

Pray about the big.

Pray about the small.

Pray about everything.

Prayer is the only thing that reaches heaven before we do.

Pray on.
Prayer *is* the work.
Worry will cease.

Chapter 9

Highly Favored, Richly Blessed

> Your husband, your children, your career, your possessions, your fame or fortune can never satisfy. Only Jesus can satisfy your heart's longing.
>
> —Jill Briscoe

I remember those piercing words coming from Jill's lips at a women's conference—oh, not in a bad way but in resounding conviction. "Yes, that is truer than true. Only Jesus can satisfy."

Easy to say. Hard to digest.

For years I stewed on how my husband wasn't living up to *my* expectations. The funny thing is that he wasn't even aware that I had specific expectations of him, so how could he possibly have lived up to them? Sadly, I had zeroed in on all the ways he wasn't satisfying my every need.

Twenty years before at our dream wedding, we had chosen 1 Corinthians 13, the familiar love passage, as our theme. The pastor personalized the scripture, replacing the word *love* with our names, so it read like this:

> Brian is patient,
> Margo is kind.
> Brian does not envy,
> Margo does not boast.
> Brian is not proud.
> Margo is not self-seeking.
> Brian is not easily angered.
> Margo keeps no record of wrongs.
> Brian always protects.
> Margo always trusts.
> Brian always hopes.
> Margo always perseveres.
> Love never fails.

He ended with these penetrating words: "May you look back at this day and see how small your love once was."

Whoa.

Reliving those words stopped me in my tracks. Not only were they poignant, but they were living and active since they were from God. I had the feeling Jesus was going to perform more intricate surgery on me—if I let Him.

I had somehow grown up with the notion that my husband was to be "my everything." My very identity. Probably because I viewed my dad like that.

The boss.
The provider.
The adviser.
The one to defer to.

How was Brian to be my everything when we were extreme opposites?

I was gregarious and enthusiastic—he, not so much.

He was analytical and logical—me, not so much.

My love language was "words of affirmation."

His love language was "acts of service."

Being with people motivated me.

He needed alone time to rejuvenate.

I was amazed by how God could take two completely different human beings, both made in His image, and create one flesh. "For this reason a man will leave his father and mother and be united to his wife, and the two will become one flesh. Therefore what God has joined together, let no one separate" (Mark 10:7–9 NIV).

The pastor had also used this verse in our wedding ceremony, noting that we were to *complete* one another, not *compete* with one another. In that completion, we would become "one."

That "completing one another" stuff turned out to be harder than I thought. My focus had to come off our differences and be placed onto Jesus. He was the equalizer. He had redeemed each of us and was making us whole in Him.

> In Jesus, it didn't matter anymore about our glaring differences.

In Jesus, it didn't matter anymore about the glaring differences in how we were raised, where we grew up, our family's personalities, or even our love languages. What *did* matter was our position in Jesus Christ. We were already highly favored and richly blessed, and we would always be.

Jesus had become my everything, so it didn't matter that Brian had come from a tiny town of less than one hundred inhabitants in northwest Iowa and that I was a big-city, New Jersey-born baby who had grown up in Madison (Madtown), Wisconsin. My family had traveled the world, while Brian's had traveled to town and back.

My household could have starred as the Greek family in *My Big, Fat Greek Wedding*. We were known to be loud, hugging, kissing, and talking over one another. A continuous assortment of friends, missionaries, neighbors, and clients came over for dinner or the weekend since we lived on a lake. If they stayed too long, Dad walked down to the boathouse and pointed at a wood-burned sign that read, "Fish and guests smell after three days!"

On the other hand, Brian's parents quietly kept to themselves. (They could have been the groom's parents in the Greek movie.) His family consisted of his dad, his mom, and him. There weren't many gatherings, church festivities, or invited company in and out of his house—except Sundays were special. They consisted of a trip to Grandpa and Grandma's farm just down the gravel road for hunting and fishing fun. Plus, a big, organic, scrumptious meal would be enjoyed by all.

On any Sunday our house was filled with the aroma of Mom's pot roast, and the dining room table swelled with Dad's invited-on-the-spot guests from church. That's when Dad instituted the "FHB Rule." Just in case there wasn't enough food prepared, Dad would lay eyes on his "3M" daughters (Marcia, Marilyn, and Margo) and mouth, "FHB." We knew the code meant "Family Hold Back." So when the peas were passed, we would take only five. Or half a dollop of mashed potatoes. Or we politely passed the serving plate of roast on by. We cut our intake of food in half, all the while knowing we'd be served Shakey's pizza later (not a bad trade-off).

My unvoiced question for Brian—*Why couldn't you be more like me?*—was no longer the undercurrent of my relationship with my husband. That hidden question had created expectations of my husband he couldn't possibly fulfill.

Thankfully, my nonnegotiable, face-to-face time with Jesus kept reeling me in. The Holy Spirit spoke into my self-centered heart, awakening His identity in me. I had become so focused on my supposed "better half" that I lost whom I belonged to. "Now I Belong to Jesus," an old hymn by Norman John Clayton (1943), which my mom used to sing (of course, she did), flooded my soul.

> Jesus, my Lord, will love me forever,
> From Him no power of evil can sever,
> He gave His life to ransom my soul,
> Now I belong to Him.
> Now I belong to Jesus,
> Jesus belongs to me,
> Not for the years of time alone
> But for eternity.

Such truth in a simple song. My identity rested in Christ alone. My past struggles didn't define me. I belonged to Him, and He belonged to me.

When I had put my faith in Christ, my security in His love was absolute. My identity was complete in Christ the moment I accepted Him as my Savior. I didn't need to go looking for my identity in anyone else. My position was in Him—in Christ. I belonged to Him. "So now there is no condemnation for those who belong to Christ Jesus. And because you belong to him. the power of the life-giving Spirit has freed you from the power of sin that leads to death" (Romans 8:1–2 NLT).

When I finally understood Jesus alone was my identity, I let my husband off the hook. (I'm sure he was relieved.) No more thinking Brian could somehow be "my everything." Jesus already was. I had lost focus for a time.

Once I was back on track, realizing Brian wasn't created to fulfill my desires, expectations, needs, or demands, I began to have false expectations of my daughters.

Yikes!

Hadn't I learned my lesson the first time?

It seemed as if I needed someone tangible, someone I could see and touch, to make me content. That certainly put a ton of pressure on them, which they could never accomplish. I went through the whole gamut of trying to find satisfaction from my husband, kids, and career. Even some good friends fell prey.

But God (my two favorite words again) won out. He reminded me that I didn't have to do anything to earn His love. "But God demonstrates His own love for us in this: While we were still sinners, Christ died for us" (Romans 5:8 NIV).

I was already highly favored and richly blessed.

All my expectations were in Christ alone. He never failed me. He's God. He can't fail. Everyone else failed me, and I failed everyone else. Only Jesus satisfied my every heart's desire. He was and still is more than enough. Consider these hymn lyrics from "No One Ever Cared for Me like Jesus" by Charles Weigle (1932).

> I would love to tell you what I think of Jesus,
> Since I found in Him a friend so strong and true.
> I would tell you how He changed my life completely,
> He did something that no other friend could do.
> No one ever cared for me like Jesus,
> There's no other friend so kind as He,
> No one else could take the sin and darkness from me;
> Oh, how much He cared for me.

When I finally came to the realization that "only Jesus can satisfy," the pressure I had placed on my precious God-given family dissipated. It's funny that when I saw myself as God saw me—already highly favored and richly blessed—because of His Son, I didn't need my husband's approval, my daughters' approval, my friend's approval, or anyone's approval for that matter. God already approved of me. I had the stamp of His Son on me. My job was to act rightly before Him. I wasn't responsible for anyone else's reactions. He lovingly reassured me, "My past struggles do not define me." Christ alone is where my identity rests.

> Christ alone is where my identity rests.

Unwavering

I now see how Jesus is
Transforming me,
Transforming my husband,
Transforming our girls,
Remaking our family
Individually and collectively.

And He wants to continually refine us to the point that we look just like Him. And that, my friends, won't be complete until we see Him face-to-face, which lets everyone off each other's hooks. I'm now able to walk in unwavering faith, knowing that no matter what comes my way, I am highly favored and richly blessed.

Thank You, Jesus, for teaching me that You alone can satisfy my every longing. Nothing and no one else can. Please forgive me for looking to everyone else for my contentment. I know I'm highly favored and richly blessed only because of my relationship with You, and my position in You will never change. I'm grateful for my husband's and children's love for You and me. I choose to leave all my expectations in You, since I will never be disappointed. I know who and whose I am—Yours.

Devotions
for Your Next Right Steps

My Identity in Christ

Still Standing
Moving to Your Forever Home
Set Free
The Right Perspective
His Masterpiece

Still Standing

> God sent me to announce the year of His grace ... to comfort all who mourn ... to give them bouquets of roses instead of ashes, messages of joy instead of news of doom, a praising heart instead of a languid spirit. Rename them "Oaks of Righteousness" planted by God to display his glory. I will sing for joy in God, explode in praise from deep in my soul! He dressed me up in a suit of salvation, he outfitted me in a robe of righteousness, as a bridegroom who puts on a tuxedo and a bride a jeweled tiara. For as the earth bursts with spring wildflowers, and as a garden cascades with blossoms, so the Master, God, brings righteousness into full bloom and puts praise on display before the nations.
>
> —Isaiah 61:1–3,10–11 (MSG)

The mighty oak, the tree that takes a beating and still stands tall. It might get a few scars from pelting hailstorms, whipping winds, and thunderstorms, but nevertheless, it stands. Oaks are the trees we marvel at when we drive by open fields, and there—in the distance—appears a single mighty oak.

Beautifully gnarled. Weather beaten. Reaching for the sky. Thick trunk. Deep, deep roots.

The major prophet Isaiah calls us "Oaks of Righteousness."

We, the people of God, because of His grace, are renamed "Oaks of Righteousness." God's gracious goal is to plant a healthy and more wind-resistant forest of mighty oaks so future storms are less devastating.

> You're not any old oak. You are an "Oak of Righteousness."

Why? "To display His glory!" To show that His fingerprints are all over these "Oaks of Righteousness!" He has outfitted you in a "suit of salvation" and a "robe of righteousness." No wonder you can weather the storms.

His salvation suit and righteousness robe comfort you and "make you sing for joy in God and explode in praise."

As the spring comes, you, O Oak of Righteousness, are prolifically budding, ready to burst out in full foliage, just like the earth is at the ready to display wildflowers and cascading blossoms of garden color.

How can you do all this? How can you weather the storms? Beautifully bud in spring? Produce full-leaf beauty in summer? Still standing when the driving winds are taking their toll?

Remember, you're not any old oak. You are an "Oak of Righteousness" God planted for a purpose, *His* purpose. To display His glory. So stand tall. You have on His healthy and wind-resistant clothes of salvation and righteousness.

The winds may beat against you, but He buffers it so He can "put you on display before the nations."

**When all is said and done,
Oaks of Righteousness are still standing
only by His grace.**

Moving to Your Forever Home

> Don't let this throw you. You trust God, don't you? Trust me. There is plenty of room for you in my Father's home. If that weren't so, would I have told you that I'm on my way to get a room ready for you? And if I'm on my way to get your room ready, I'll come back and get you so you can live where I live. And you already know the road I'm taking.
>
> —John 14:1–4 (MSG)

Don't you love it when your room is all done up for you? Ready for you to enjoy? Don't you enjoy that wonderful feeling when you open the door and the room is perfectly clean and inviting, with fresh towels and crisp linens? It speaks aloud to enter and delight in it.

Imagine the room Jesus is preparing just for you in His Father's house—heaven. Incomparable. Perfect in every way. I mean, if Jesus is the Preparer of your room—and He is—then it will be prepared perfectly with you in mind.

There is going to be so much rejoicing and gladness when you arrive in heaven that your room won't be the first thing on your mind. This is the Father's big house. And Jesus is personally escorting you from your earthly home to your forever home.

You were made for this.

You have accepted Jesus's truth. "I am the way, the truth and the life. No one comes to the Father except through me" (John 14:6 NIV). The Bible calls you a "citizen of heaven" now. You're just waiting for your appointed time to move into the Father's home.

Psalm 139 tells us "that every day has been ordained before one of them came to be." So Jesus knows your moving day, and He is personally getting your room ready for your arrival—not a minute too soon or too late. His timing is perfect.

Think about it: you're never moving out of this grand and grace-filled home. This isn't a temporary abode. This is your place for all eternity. Forever. Always. Never ending. "As for man, his days are like grass; as a flower of the field, so he flourishes. For the wind passes over it, and it is gone, And its place remembers it no more. But the mercy of the Lord is from everlasting to everlasting on those who fear Him" (Psalm 103:15–17 NKJV).

> You're never moving out of this grand and grace-filled home.

You know your room will be filled with the things that really matter. I'm sure there will be a huge welcome basket full of fruit, the fruit that never decays. This is real fruit the Holy Spirit provided in and through you while on earth: "love, joy, peace, patience, kindness, goodness, faithfulness, gentleness and self-control" (Galatians 5:22–23).

Now that fruit has become completely ripe for you to enjoy. Just the fact that you will live where Jesus lives will be enough joy for all eternity.

A "Welcome Home" sign, surely written in Jesus's blood, will be hanging on your door. This sign assures you that, since you were abiding with Jesus on earth, you will abide in His abode forever. While on earth, you walked by faith and not by sight, but now your eyes see Him in all His glory.

When I arrive, I'm sure I will notice that Jesus added little personal touches to my room like a vase of bird-of-paradise (my favorite flower) and a tray of guacamole and blue chips (my favorite treat to share with you).

One day you will change addresses and move to heaven forever with Jesus.

Set Free

> I write this, dear children, to guide you out of sin. But if anyone does sin, we have a Priest-Friend in the presence of the Father: Jesus Christ, righteous Jesus. When he served as a sacrifice for our sins, he solved the sin problem for good—not only ours, but the whole world's.
>
> —1 John 2:1–2 (MSG)

It seems like no one likes to use the word *sin* nowadays. If you can rename it, you will, using synonyms such as *deficiencies, errors, imperfections, mistakes, shortcomings,* or even *sowing wild oats.* Then *sin* doesn't seem as bad.

However, until we realize sin *is* bad and that we need to be saved from it, we will go on our merry little way, which leads to destruction. "For the wages of sin is death, but the free gift of God is eternal life in Christ Jesus our Lord" (Romans 6:23 ESV).

Sin is actually spelled s-I-n—little *s*, big *I*, little *n*. Why is that? As long as you keep *I* on the throne, you're gonna sin. "My wants, my rights! I don't need to listen to anyone else, including God."

Those are the thoughts of someone on a slippery slope with that willful, deliberate attitude.

The beloved disciple, John, was writing this to "guide us out of sin," but if anyone does sin (and he knew we would, for "all have sinned and fall short of the glory of God" [Romans 3:23]), we have a Priest-Friend in the presence of the Father, Jesus Christ.

What a promise!

What deliverance!

What a Savior!

Jesus has already solved the sin problem for good. Forever. Perfect, sinless Jesus. The Son of God, the one who knew no sin but became sin for us.

"For our sake he made him to be sin who knew no sin, so that in him we might become the righteousness of God" (2 Corinthians 5:21 ESV). We already have the solution to sin:

> Jesus has already solved the sin problem for good.

the Savior, righteous Jesus. He is yours for the taking, but you first need to believe you *need* a Savior—that you need to be saved from your sin.

God has already provided a way out of sin, but when we don't see sin as sin, we excuse our behavior. We blame others, rationalize, and pretend we are good enough. *After all, I'm not like that person. I would never do that.*

But God says, "For whoever keeps the whole law and yet stumbles at one point is guilty of breaking all of it" (James 2:10 NIV).

I want to be guided out of s-I-n. I'm so grateful that Jesus took the hit for me. I can now enter God's presence through my Priest-Friend, Jesus. He took not only my sin but also the whole world's.

> This is how much God loved the world:
> He gave his Son, his one and only Son.
> And this is why: so that no one need be

destroyed; by believing in him, anyone can have a whole and lasting life. God didn't go to all the trouble of sending his Son merely to point an accusing finger, telling the world how bad it was. He came to help, to put the world right again. Anyone who trusts in him is acquitted; anyone who refuses to trust him has long since been under the death sentence without knowing it. And why? Because of that person's failure to believe in the one-of-a-kind Son of God when introduced to him."

(John 3:16–18 MSG)

Jesus's sacrifice on the cross solved the sin problem for good.

The Right Perspective

> You yourselves know how plainly I told you, "I am not the Messiah. I am only here to prepare the way for him." It is the bridegroom who marries the bride, and the bridegroom's friend is simply glad to stand with him and hear his vows. Therefore, I am filled with joy at his success. He must become greater and greater, and I must become less and less.
>
> —John 3:28–30 (NLT)

John the Baptist had the right perspective. His job had been telling everyone who was within earshot that the Messiah, God's Son, Jesus, was coming. And then, once they believed, he wanted to baptize them as an outward profession of an inward confession.

However, many thought he might be the Messiah, but John the Baptist made sure to set them right. "I am not the Messiah. I am only here to prepare the way for Him."

As John the Baptist was baptizing people, his close friends noticed that Jesus (the one John had been preparing the way for) was now baptizing people just up the river, and they were starting to take up an offense for him. After all, this baptizing job belonged to their buddy, John the Baptist. (His name even described his position.)

John the Baptist quickly gave them a word picture to help them understand. It had to do with a wedding and the positioning of the bridegroom and the best man. "The bridegroom marries the bride. The best man is simply glad to stand with him and hear his vows."

You've probably been to a wedding, been in a wedding, or the wedding was your own. It's obvious the spotlight is on the bride and the bridegroom. If the maid of honor or best man drew attention to herself or himself instead of tending to the bride and groom, you would be abhorred. You would become unsettled in your seat, thinking, *This is their day. They are the ones committing their vows to one another. Not you!*

John the Baptist was telling the people that the real deal was here. "He, the Messiah, has come. He is fulfilling His work given Him by the Father. He is the Ultimate Bridegroom who has come for His bride. So pay attention to Him. I just paved the way. He is here. It's all about Him and not me!"

And that, my friends, is how we are to live. Jesus must become greater and greater, and I must become less and less. It's all about Him on the throne of my life and me getting off it to attend to Him. It's about knowing Him and His ways. It's about becoming more and more like Him and less like my putrid self.

> It's all about Him on the throne of my life and me getting off it.

And you know what happens then? We will say, like John the Baptist exclaimed, "Therefore, I am filled with joy at His success."

**It's not about my success.
It's all about His success in me.**

His Masterpiece

> Since this is the kind of life we have chosen, the life of the Spirit, let us make sure that we do not just hold it as an idea in our heads or a sentiment in our hearts, but work out its implications in every detail of our lives. That means we will not compare ourselves with each other as if one of us were better and another worse. We have far more interesting things to do with our lives. Each of us is an original.
>
> —Galatians 5:25–26 (MSG)

Don't you love originals? An original piece of artwork? An original glass-blown vase? An original Granny Square afghan your nana crocheted just for you? An original painting proudly signed by your first-grader?

> The best originals are you and me.

Well, the best "originals" are—drum roll—you and me. Yeah, God made each of us as "an original." You have your own unique DNA. The Holy Spirit gifted each of us for His special purpose.

You can't be mistaken for anyone else in the whole universe. You are an original God made. He's placed His personal, divine autograph on you, and you were made in His image. He's proud of His masterpiece: you.

This means we need to treat God-made originals with tender-loving care. You don't just throw an original into the trash. Originals are carefully tended and placed, since they are highly esteemed. No price can be put on an original. No one can replace an original. Once it's gone, it's irreplaceable.

The apostle Paul told us that since we have chosen to live by the Spirit of God, our actions toward other originals need to be as He would act. This living-by-the-Spirit thing isn't head knowledge, but it's worked out with the "originals" in our daily interactions.

That means that since we are each an "original" of God's handiwork, we dare not compare ourselves, saying, "I'm better than that original!"

You are not. You are unique. You are made in His image.

You are an amazing original of God, but you are not better than the next original. You have been given different gifts and talents that are to intertwine with other original God-given gifts and talents. That's harmony among the originals.

Can you imagine an original oil painting, such as Leonardo de Vinci's *Mona Lisa,* saying to an original sculpted statue, such as Michelangelo's *David,* "I am more of an original than you! I am better than you"? That's ridiculous.

We should acknowledge, enjoy, be grateful for, and actually welcome one another's God-given attributes and gifts. There should be no comparisons.

So don't compare yourself with another as if you are better than the other. Live formatively, not comparatively. God created you to do far more interesting things with your life.

Each of us is a God original.

Chapter 10

Knowing Jesus

Personally, passionately, powerfully, and preeminently.

"It doesn't matter what I think. It matters what Jesus thinks."

I uttered those words to a friend, who was struggling, as she walked through an unexpected divorce. She wanted my advice. She wanted me to tell her what to do. I was tempted to give her my opinion, but it would flare up only from my skewed frame of reference. After all, years earlier I had experienced my own horrific divorce.

It would have been so easy to have jumped on her bandwagon, joining in blasting her husband. Then came my two favorite words, "But God!"

He had brought me to the end of sharing my biased opinions and instead centered me on His opinions, which are from His Word. Besides, His words are life changing and mine—well, they aren't. "For the Word of God is alive and active. Sharper than any double-edged sword, it penetrates even to dividing the soul and spirit, joints and marrow; it judges the thoughts and attitudes of the heart" (Hebrews 4:12 NIV).

I dug into the Bible with my friend, praying she would stand on His promises, which are powerful, comforting, and convicting.

I stood in the gap. I kept going back to His promises, noting that she could stand on them or choose to fall back on her feelings. I reminded her that "faith is not a feeling." Rather, it's faith that starves our fears, but it was up to her to attend her own pity party or come and eat at the banquet table God had prepared. His desire for us is to taste and see that He is good. "Taste and see that the Lord is good; blessed is the one who takes refuge in him" (Psalm 34:8 NIV).

It was such a privilege to share God's Word with her to "give her hope and a future," as the Bible promises us in Jeremiah 29:11, but I could only passionately teach her what I had already eaten off my own God-served plate. As I look back, He graciously served me many courses, from appetizers to desserts, but I'm pretty sure it has been more than any ten-course meal I consumed in Paris.

> It has taken a lifetime.
> A lifetime of sitting at His table.
> Sometimes chowing down.
> Other times just snacking.
> Maybe only nibbling.
> But always absorbing.
> And digesting.

Dinner is so much better when you have a relationship with the one at your table. That's the only way you can sit at the Father's banquet table—through a personal relationship with His Son, Jesus.

He was always inviting me. All I had to do was accept the offer.

As I conversed with Jesus, I noticed that I was falling more and more in love. I couldn't take my eyes off Him. His beauty. His demeanor. He could stare deeply into my soul. My relationship grew from knowing Him personally to finding an overflowing excitement. I could hardly contain myself as I told others at the table about what Jesus was doing in my life. I was white-hot passionate about our relationship and noticed others were following me right to the Father's banquet table, since I was making them hungry for what I had.

> My relationship grew from knowing Him personally to finding an overflowing excitement.

As the Father served me the next course, some of the "sides" weren't very palatable. Seriously, I had a very hard time swallowing, since they tasted like lima beans or were as dry as shredded wheat.

However, as I continued to digest them, I noticed more and more people coming to sit with me at His banquet table. I overheard their conversations. They had been watching me "keep on keepin' on" through the unsavory course. Scooting up next to my chair, they asked how I could have possibly continued, especially without grumbling.

Discussion continued on how I depended on His power, not my own. I explained that when I felt I could not go on, the Holy Spirit, who lived in me, was my power. And as Oswald Chambers wrote, "He doesn't give you the power ... He is your power."

I opened the book that was prominently displayed on the banquet table and read aloud.

> Greater is he that is in you, than he that is in the world. (1 John 4:4 KJV)

> I pray that the eyes of your heart may be enlightened in order that you may know the hope to which he has called you, the riches of his glorious inheritance in his holy people, and his incomparably great power for us who believe. That power is the same as the mighty strength he exerted when he raised Christ from the dead and seated him at his right hand in the heavenly realms, far above all rule and authority, power and dominion, and every name that is invoked, not only in the present age but also in the one to come. (Ephesians 1:18–22 NIV)

> Now to him who is able to do immeasurably more than all we ask or imagine, according to his power that is at work within us, to him be glory in the church and in Christ Jesus throughout all generations, forever and ever! Amen. (Ephesians 3:20–21 NIV)

I closed the book and noticed there wasn't a dry eye at the table. Jesus had that kind of I'm-so-proud-of-you smile curling His lips. I had gone from a personal to a passionate to a powerful relationship with Him. It took the tough and chewy side courses to bring out His flavor in me. It sure didn't happen during the cake-and-ice cream celebratory dessert times.

I settled into the next course. The main entree had arrived, eye appealing, succulent, and aromatic. I relished every bite, never wanting it to end.

I noticed Jesus was now seated at the head of the banquet table. As we dined throughout the evening, His location seemed perfect. I had never been more content and I knew it wasn't because of the delectable food.

He was now in the place of authority at the table. He had taken preeminence. No wonder I was satisfied. He ruled over every detail of each course that was served.

> I noticed Jesus was now seated at the head of the banquet table.

The savory and unsavory: the savory gift of two children through God's best plan along with the unsavory years of infertility issues.

The delicious and the disagreeable: the delicious satisfaction of a child with the ease of success and the disagreeable years of parenting struggles.

The gratifying and the repulsive: the gratifying match of two imperfect souls to a perfect God, and the repulsive memories of an abusive past marriage.

The scrumptious and the sickening: the scrumptious dessert of my sweet mom's prayers and the sickening reality of how long it had taken me to answer the invitation to His table.

However, now I willingly accepted each course from His loving hand, knowing He was preeminent over every detail. I trusted that He wouldn't serve me anything that didn't fill me up. As I took in His nourishment, I knew I was experiencing the fullness of joy I was created to know, with Jesus seated at the head of every area of my life.

Father God, what a privilege to sit at Your banquet table all my days. Jesus, thank You for inviting me personally. I'm eternally grateful.

Holy Spirit, Your power is how I keep standing on the promises. Even though my courses of life may never change, teach me to trust, without fail, in the changeless God. I trust that You, the triune God, will always do exceedingly, abundantly more than I could ask or think. I love You.

Thank You for teaching me to be steady, fixed, resolved, constant, steadfast, enduring, abiding, unswerving, untiring, and relentless.

May I be unwavering as I keep on learning to do the next right thing in my walk with You.

Devotions
for Your Next Right Steps

Standing on His Promises

Strong and Able Faith
Go after the One
Promises that Cannot Fail
Supernatural Harvest
No Pinky Promises Here
Beaming with Pride

Strong and Able Faith

Those of us who are strong and able in the faith need to step in and lend a hand to those who falter, and not just do what is most convenient for us. Strength is for service, not status. Each one of us needs to look after the good of the people around us, asking ourselves, "How can I help?" That's exactly what Jesus did. He didn't make it easy for himself by avoiding people's troubles, but waded right in and helped out. God wants the combination of his steady, constant calling and warm, personal counsel in Scripture to come to characterize us, keeping us alert for whatever he will do.

—Romans 15:1–2, 4 (MSG)

Do you help others who are struggling? Who have faltered? Who need a strong arm to lean on? The only way you'll be able to help is by *you* being strong and able—not physically but like a muscleman (or woman) in your faith.

You need to be further along in your faith than the person you are helping. You need a faith that knows that you know God always keeps His promises. With an unwavering faith like that, you simply lead the hurting soul back to life, just like Jesus did. He walked right into a person's problem and asked, "How can I help?" He didn't make it easy on Himself by avoiding their troubles.

He knew what they needed. He knew that, whatever it was, He had the answer. He had the promise.

That's when our strong and able faith says, "No matter what your trouble, I will take you to the answer. His name is Jesus! And He hasn't failed me yet."

The reason you can share such hope is because you know what He has done for you. Your faith has grown leaps and bounds as you search the scriptures. You can give personal counsel as you lead others to His Word.

> The reason you can share such hope is because you know what He has done for you.

The key to actually helping others isn't about giving them *your* advice. It's about using your grown-up faith and leading them to God's Word. He will give them His perfect advice, just like He has done with you.

Then you'll be characterized as a godly helper, walking in God's strength, unconcerned about your status. Just one who is known for your warm, personal counsel from God's Word.

As you are helping the next person and the next and the next, you are on alert.

**You see how God is working.
You're ready for whatever
He has for you to do.**

Go after the One

> Go easy on those who hesitate in the faith. Go after those who take the wrong way. Be tender with sinners, but not soft on sin. The sin itself stinks to high heaven.
>
> —Jude 1:22–23 (MSG)

Notice that we are exhorted to
"Go easy,"
"Go after," and
"Be tender."

Those who are reluctant or having doubts in their faith? Go easy on them. Come alongside them, walk with them, living out your faith in the ever-faithful God. They will eventually desire to do the same.

> Those who are on the wrong path? Go after them.

Those who are on the wrong path? Go after them. If friends are lost and wandering? Send out a rescue team to find them. Post a missing-person report. Go on the initiative to find them, just like Jesus did with the one lost sheep. Ninety-nine out of one-hundred were safe in the fold. (Those are pretty good odds but not for Jesus.) He goes after the one who needs Him most. He finds him or her and brings that person back to safety. We should follow His example.

For those who are sinning? Be tender with them. What? Tender on sin? No. Tender with the person who is sinning but not with the actual sin itself.

Let's remind ourselves of what sin is. It is "any reprehensible or regrettable action, behavior, lapse; great fault or offense." The sin is what needs to be dealt with, and Jesus already paid for the sin debt on the cross. Past, present, and future sin. Hallelujah! The one doing the sinning needs to know he or she can be forgiven by God and by you. He or she can be set free in Jesus to go and sin no more.

How would the person learn this marvelous truth if you weren't tender with him or her? If you didn't love what God loves? The sinner. And hate what God hates? The actual sin. Romans 5:8 says, *"But God demonstrated His love for us in this, while we were yet sinners, He died for us"* (emphasis mine).

Talk about God's tenderness. Talk about God's mercy. We are to pass along His tenderness, which leads the sinner to repentance. That means he or she wants to turn around and go the exact opposite way he or she had been going. The person desires to leave the sin life and embrace the tender forgiveness of Jesus. In Jeremiah 31:3, we are reminded that "He draws us with His loving kindness." Always!

> We are to pass along His tenderness.

But the sin itself? Well, that stinks! It stinks up the one doing the sinning. It stinks up the atmosphere around the person sinning. It pukes that horrific odor onto others close by the person sinning. "The sin itself stinks to high heaven."

We shouldn't condone sin, or we'll start stinking too. No, our focus should be like the Savior's—tender with sinne.rs but not soft on sin.

**We have received God's tenderness.
How can we extend it to others?**

Promises that Cannot Fail

> "When you call on me, when you come and pray to me, I'll listen. When you come looking for me, you'll find me. Yes, when you get serious about finding me and want it more than anything else, I'll make sure you won't be disappointed." God's Decree. "I'll turn things around for you ... You can count on it."
>
> —Jeremiah 29:12, 14 (MSG)

Jeremiah tells us of God's personal promises to His people, to you and me. He decreed it. It is so. We can depend on Him as if our very lives depended on His decrees. (And quite frankly, they do.) God's promises will stand the test of time and then some. They are for all time. They will never fail. They are birthed from God Almighty. They can't fail.

The prophet Jeremiah tells us of God's decrees.

1. He will listen.
2. He is able to be found.
3. He will not disappoint.
4. He will turn things around.
5. He is dependable.

1. He will listen. My heart leaps for joy! My God will listen, turn His ear toward me. He cares enough about me to actually listen to me. In this frenetic world,

people may hear me, but very few listen to my heart. But God does, and that's all that matters.

2. He is able to be found. Have you ever tried to get ahold of someone you needed to talk to, but he or she was nowhere to be found? You call, text, e-mail, personal message on Facebook, and show up at his or her home, but you keep missing him or her? Not with God. He is able to be found. He is at the ready.

3. He won't disappoint. Everyone else will fail you—will disappoint you—but God promises He won't. He cannot. He's God. He's not talking about all your wants. He knows what you need even before you do, and it's Him. He promises that He will never disappoint you.

4. He will turn things around. Ever been traveling the wrong way on a road trip? Oh, I have. I remember driving 150 miles in the wrong direction as my parents snoozed in the car. Upon my dad's waking, he guided me on the right road. He turned things around for me and set me in the right direction. The same is true of our heavenly Father.

5. He is dependable. What God says He does. You can depend on Him. If you have an earthly friend you can trust to do what he or she says he or she will do and be where he or she says he or she will be, then you are blessed. But to know God is dependable, that you can rely on Him for everything, and that He has decreed it—that is heavenly.

So, if God has decreed all these promises to His people (and He has), how do we receive them? How do God's promises become my personal promises?

Easy. He tells us. He wants us to partake. This is a two-way street.

He beckons us to "call on Me. Come and pray to Me. Come look for Me. Get serious about finding Me. Want Me more than anything else."

That's it. He *is* the Promise Maker, the Promise Giver. I am the promise receiver.

> He is the Promise Maker.

Actively pursue an ongoing relationship with the one I love and trust.

Supernatural Harvest

> Don't be misled: No one makes a fool of God. What a person plants, he will harvest. The person who plants selfishness, ignoring the needs of others—ignoring God!—harvests a crop of weeds. All he'll have to show for his life is weeds! But the one who plants in response to God, letting God's Spirit do the growth work in him, harvests a crop of real life, eternal life. So let's not allow ourselves to get fatigued doing good. At the right time we will harvest a good crop if we don't give up or quit.
>
> —Galatians 6:7–9 (MSG)

Obvious Fact #1: What you plant you harvest.

If you plant an apple seed, you reap an apple tree that bears apples. It certainly won't bear oranges.

Every year in spring, my in-laws would plant their huge garden. And every fall, their harvest was faithful to the seeds that were planted. Beans, tomatoes, corn, zucchini, and cucumbers burst through the soil right where they were planted. No surprises.

So why is it that the apostle Paul needed to remind us that it's the same obvious principle with you and me? If you plant selfishness, you will reap only weeds in your life. If you don't care about others or God, your life will produce nothing but weeds (that invasive species in the garden that springs up and chokes out the good harvest).

Why can't we understand that, if we're all about ourselves, our lives will produce nothing but weeds? Why do we not *want* to understand that? Producing weeds is worse than producing nothing at all.

Weeds are a nemesis to a good crop. They will choke out the seedlings of the intended good harvest. That's just what selfishness does. It strangles the good that could have been produced.

> Weeds are a nemesis to a good crop.

If you sow to the flesh, you will reap nothing but a throwaway life. But if you listen and respond to God's Spirit living in you, instead of letting your own selfish desires take over like weeds, you will harvest a crop of real life, eternal life. Life that makes a difference now and for all eternity.

The harvest of living this kind of life has dividends now *and* later. This is an eternal harvest. It's a supernatural harvest, since "God's Spirit is doing the growth work in you." The harvest goes on forever.

So, if we were to sum up what Paul was saying, we have to keep on keepin' on doing good ("letting God's Spirit do the growth work in us"), then—at just the right time (God's always-perfect timing)—we will harvest a good crop (if we don't give up or quit).

Obvious Fact #2: What you plant you harvest.

Yep, we are always going back to this truth. You can't make a fool of God.

Be very careful about what you are planting.

No Pinky Promises Here

> So, what do you think? With God on our side like this, how can we lose? The One who died for us—who was raised to life for us!—is in the presence of God at this very moment sticking up for us. Do you think anyone is going to be able to drive a wedge between us and Christ's love for us? There is no way! Not trouble, not hard times, not hatred, not hunger, not homelessness, not bullying threats, not backstabbing, not even the worst sins listed in Scripture ... None of this fazes us because Jesus loves us. I'm absolutely convinced that nothing—nothing living or dead, angelic or demonic, today or tomorrow, high or low, thinkable or unthinkable—absolutely nothing can get between us and God's love because of the way that Jesus our Master has embraced us.
>
> —Romans 8:31, 34, 36–39 (MSG)

Do you need a pep talk? Well, reread the above truths from the apostle Paul. What encouragement! "With God on our side like this, how can we lose?"

God+Me=A majority. There's your equation if you have a relationship with the one (Jesus) who died for you and was raised to life for you (and is sticking up for you in the presence of His Father God). That's way enough for me.

Almighty, merciful God is on my side because I am His child through His Son Jesus's death and resurrection. I am embraced by Jesus's love. No one—and that means no one—will be able to drive a wedge between Jesus and me.

Nope.

Nada.

No one.

Not any trouble that comes along.

Not any hard times that may occur.

Not any hunger that might arise.

Not if I am homeless for a while.

Not when someone bullies me.

Not even when someone stabs me in the back with his or her words.

Not even if the worst sins mentioned in the Bible are committed against me. Nope, nothing—and no one can separate me from the love of Christ. All this stuff doesn't even faze me since I am kept by His love.

And if that's not enough of a pep talk, there's more:

Not anything living or dead—that pretty much covers all creatures, including you and me.

Not angels or demons—that pretty much covers the good and evil spirit worlds.

> Absolutely nothing can get between us and God's love.

Not today or tomorrow—that pretty much covers now and forever.

Not anything high or low—that pretty much covers above and under the earth.

Not anything thinkable or unthinkable—okay, now this covers it all.

Absolutely nothing can get between us and God's love because of the way Jesus, our Master, has embraced us. So, if you're in trouble or hard times or hungry or homeless or experiencing threats, bullying, or backstabbing or (fill in the blank), Jesus loves you. He is sticking up for you. He is on your side. You *cannot* lose. You already have victory through Him.

Gaze at your Savior. Bask in His deep love. He promises that nothing and no one can separate you from His great love.

Steep in your God promise.

Beaming with Pride

Do your best. Work from the heart for your real Master, for God, confident that you'll get paid in full when you come into your inheritance. Keep in mind always that the ultimate Master you're serving is Christ. The sullen servant who does shoddy work will be held responsible. Being a follower of Jesus doesn't cover up bad work.

—Colossians 3:22–25 (MSG)

Do you always do your best work? Giving every task your all? Including menial things, such as picking up that paper towel you dropped on the public restroom floor? (Or do you think no one will see—and besides, it's their job to clean it up?)

Then that old wristband comes to mind: WWJD? Those hauntingly familiar words flood your thoughts: *What would Jesus do?*

It's not just in the big picture of work, such as pursuing your career, cleaning your home, landscaping your yard, volunteering at church, serving on a mission trip, or studying for an exam, that you are to do your best. No, it's in the individual tasks that comprise the big-picture work that really count.

All tasks—the ones you like to do *and* the ones you don't—need to be approached as though you are working for the Lord. Remember, He is your ultimate

Master. He is the one you are working for, not for mere man. And that mind-set makes a huge difference in your attitude and quality of work. Then, and only then, will you be working from your heart.

Plus, there's a delightful bonus. God will pay you in full when you come into your inheritance. There's a bit of time delay in the payment, but oh—it will be worth it. So don't focus on just the here and now as you work. Focus on Thee day—the day when you see Jesus face to face.

> Don't just focus on the here and now.

You may not be receiving the wage you desire, the promotions you deserve, or the appreciation from others (including your family), but God sees all. He sees your sacrificial, good-attitude work. He sees you doing your best without any recognition. He sees you doing the next right thing, whether you want to or not. He sees that your feelings are obeying your faith.

And He, as your real Master, is beaming with pride as you are showing all those around you that you are a follower of Jesus Christ.

He can hardly wait to lavish on you your full inheritance.

Addendum

A Note to Readers

And gratitude for unwavering support.

Jesus doesn't give you "Ten Rules to Follow For a Happier Life," but He does give you a gift, a measure of faith that will be tested along life's way.

"Consider it pure joy, my brothers and sisters, whenever you face trials of many kinds, because you know that the testing of your faith produces perseverance. Let perseverance finish its work so that you may be mature and complete, not lacking anything" (James 1:2–4 NIV).

That's unwavering faith.

I pray, as you walked through my life story devotional, that it became very apparent with every test or trial how my faith continued to grow up.

Sometimes just a little.

Sometimes by leaps and bounds.

But always maturing. Always moving forward, since my desire is to become more and more like Jesus and less and less like my putrid self.

My husband and I have been walking in the "joy of the Lord as our strength" in our marriage for thirty years.

Our oldest daughter, Becca, age twenty-three, is pursuing her master's degree in biomedical sciences while working full-time in a pediatric gastrointestinal diagnostic lab. It is so sweet to see her own her own faith and watch her grow up in Him.

Tori, our nineteen-year-old, is proudly serving in the US Navy. She is stationed in Norfolk, VA, preparing to be deployed (and then off to ports unknown). We are so grateful she knows the truth of Jesus and is pursuing her dream of serving our country in the military.

My precious mom moved to heaven thirteen years ago at the age of eighty-eight. She gave away her life so I could find mine. She taught me how to live for Christ and how to die in Him. Her faith was unwavering.

Instead of attending our annual Wisconsin Badger football game together, my dad moved to heaven in his sleep. He was only sixty-seven. He was a changed man because of Christ.

My father-in-law, just three months after he and his wife moved from Iowa to be closer to us, moved to heaven suddenly. Thankfully, He had come to Jesus twenty years before.

Still keeping on, my mother-in-law is alive and well at age eighty-six, and she lives in an independent senior living facility only three miles from our home. Twenty-three years after her botched back surgery, she is still sharp as a tack and still a follower of Jesus.

My sisters, Marcia and Marilyn, the other two Ms of the 3M sisters, and their husbands, adult kids, and grandkids are all doing well. They are such a blessing to me and my family.

And I can't forget about our family that is four-legged.

Willow Joy, our ninety-pound collie, keeps me laughing. My walking sidekick has a personality that doesn't quit, and she is a gift from God. Lovely Lily, our rescued American paint, has been a sweet part of our family for the past thirteen years—and hopefully for many more to come. Plus, for my husband's birthday, we added to our family a tricolor collie puppy, Cedar Grace, who has enough energy for all of us.

Through it all, I desire to do the next right thing in my walk with God so no matter what comes along, my faith will be unwavering.

About Margo Fieseler

As a child, Margo's family moved from New Jersey to Madison, and she's been a proud Wisconsinite ever since. Despite a marketing career (which would ultimately span twenty years), her life really began (to the full) when she accepted Christ at age thirty-one. Following her life in marketing, she worked as a DJ for five years with the Christian radio station The Fish.

Today, she is a disciple of Jesus very cleverly disguised as a wife, mother, YMCA board member, and passionate teacher of the Word at the head of Margo Fieseler Ministries in southern Wisconsin. When she isn't teaching Bible studies and personal reflections, you can find Margo and her family skiing (on snow or water), kayaking, boating, enjoying music around the piano, or—unwaveringly—walking her furry, four-legged friends.

To learn more about Margo and her ministry, visit Margofieseler.com or connect with her on social media.

CPSIA information can be obtained
at www.ICGtesting.com
Printed in the USA
FFHW02n1913160918